CW01667419

Wagner's *Parsifal*

THE JOURNEY OF A SOUL

Peter Bassett has been studying Wagner's works for nearly forty years, after first encountering them in radio broadcasts from the Bayreuth Festival. He pursued his interest in these works while serving in Australian embassies in Western Europe, Eastern Europe, Asia and the Pacific. It was during a diplomatic posting in Burma in the early eighties that his interest in Buddhism was kindled, and he brings this to bear on his analysis of *Parsifal*. Wagner was deeply interested in Buddhism and drew on it for many of his ideas in his final work. Peter Bassett's *A Ring for the Millennium: A Guide to Wagner's Der Ring des Nibelungen* received considerable acclaim for its clarity and readability, and has now also been published in Finnish.

This book was written to accompany The State Opera of South Australia's 2001 Adelaide production of *Parsifal*.

By the same author

A Ring for the Millennium: A Guide to Wagner's Der Ring des Nibelungen

Wagner's *Parsifal*

THE JOURNEY OF A SOUL

Peter Bassett

Wakefield Press

Wakefield Press
Box 2266
Kent Town
South Australia 5071

First published 2000

Copyright © Peter Bassett 2000

All rights reserved. This book is copyright. Apart from any fair dealing for the purposes of private study, research, criticism or review, as permitted under the Copyright Act, no part may be reproduced without written permission.
Enquiries should be addressed to the publisher.

Designed and typeset by Michael Deves, Adelaide
Printed and bound by Hyde Park Press, Adelaide

Cover illustration: *Parsifal* by Peter Bassett

National Library of Australia
Cataloguing-in-Publication entry

Bassett, Peter.
Wagner's Parsifal: the journey of a soul.
Includes index

ISBN 1 86254 512 X

1. Wagner, Richard, 1813–1883 – Criticism and interpretaton.
2. Wagner, Richard, 1813–1883. Parsifal.
I. Title.

782.1

Parsifal

The medieval vision of Christ. An eleventh-century stained-glass image from the Abbey Church of Wissembourg, Alsace, now in the Musée de l'Oeuvre Notre-Dame, Strasbourg.

Contents

A romantic encounter amidst the flowers. A thirteenth-century anticipation of the delights of Klingsor's garden. From the Manessa Codex.

Foreword

Wagner called *Parsifal* his 'farewell to the world' and, in many ways, it is a summing up of themes and ideas that had preoccupied him for much of his life. In July 1882, barely seven months before his death, *Parsifal* was performed for the first time in the revolutionary theatre at Bayreuth – another of his legacies. It is difficult to think of any other artist who accomplished more, or had such an impact on music and the theatre arts.

In *Parsifal*, the music and the drama are inseparable. To hear the music is to know the drama. However, with a work of such subtlety and wealth of ideas, it is useful to know something of the motivations of its creator and the circumstances of its creation. An understanding of the relationship between the sources and the finished work, and the extent to which imagery and even language is carried from one to the other, can be especially insightful. To be able to think about the text and music in advance or reflect upon it afterwards, adds immeasurably to the experience of a performance. That is why this book, like Peter Bassett's earlier volume on the *Ring* published to coincide with the 1998 Adelaide production, is so valuable, and why I commend it to all who would know better this supremely beautiful work by Richard Wagner.

S.R.C. Phillips

Stephen Phillips
General Director, The State Opera of South Australia

... every time I glance at the

score of Parsifal,

I say to myself:

this is the sublime one.

ARTURO TOSCANINI

PREFACE

The Grail and the Spear

Parsifal is a story of Christian virtues and aspirations. However, its details are not drawn from biblical sources but from medieval romances such as Wolfram von Eschenbach's thirteenth-century poem *Parzival,* and from the teachings and legends of the Buddha.

The Grail is one of two central objects in the story and possesses mystical powers, including the ability to prolong life, to be a source of food and drink, and to bring general well-being to all who come within its presence. These miraculous qualities are not of Wagner's invention but derive from medieval legends that are, in turn, inspired by classical, Celtic and oriental mythologies. The Grail is variously described by medieval authors as: a dish or platter (Chrétien de Troyes), the cup used at the Last Supper (Robert de Boron), and a talismanic stone (Wolfram von Eschenbach). It is not mentioned in the New Testament and has never been recognised in any ecclesiastical tradition – which is hardly surprising since its origins are more pagan than Christian.

The second important object in *Parsifal* is the Holy Spear, the so-called Spear of Longinus, used to wound Christ on the Cross. Wagner gave it a prominent place in his text, as a focus for Parsifal's quest. A Holy Spear is mentioned in some medieval stories, but both Chrétien and Wolfram refer to a 'bleeding lance'. Again, this has its origins in pagan (Celtic) symbolism. The spear to which passing reference is made in St John's Gospel appears to have been a very ordinary soldier's weapon for which no special claims were made in the Bible, either before or after the wounding.

Therefore, *Parsifal* is no more a 'sacred' work of art than it is a 'historical' one. But it is an exceptionally beautiful and moving drama of inspiration and despair, strength and frailty, and a search for the divine in a far from perfect world.

Adelaide
January 2000

Synopsis of Parsifal

A Festival Play for the Dedication of the Stage in three acts
By Richard Wagner

Act One

It is daybreak in a shady forest near Montsalvat, the castle of the Grail. Amfortas, the ruler of the kingdom of the Grail is soon to take his bath in the lake. The knight Gurnemanz and two young squires awake to prepare for the king's arrival. We learn from knights accompanying the king that he can find no relief from a wound in his side that refuses to heal. Kundry, a wild-eyed, demon-like woman bursts into the clearing bringing exotic remedies for the ailing Amfortas. When the king is carried in on his litter he is in agony and despair. He concludes bitterly that his only hope is 'an Innocent Fool made wise through compassion', whose coming has been foretold. He thinks he knows him already, he says – his name is Death! He thanks Kundry for her gift and her loyalty.

After the king and his retinue have moved to the lake, Gurnemanz rebukes the squires for their uncharitable behaviour towards Kundry. She has become a servant of the Grail Knights, he says, perhaps to atone for some guilt in a former life. He goes on to explain how the wound of Amfortas had been inflicted by the sorcerer Klingsor with the Holy Spear, the same spear that had been used to wound the body of Christ after his crucifixion. Klingsor had seized the spear from its guardian, Amfortas, when he had succumbed to the wiles of a beautiful woman. The spear and the Grail had been entrusted originally to Titurel, Amfortas's father, who had assembled a company of the purest knights to guard them. Klingsor, himself a knight, had been excluded from this company because of his sinful ways. In desperation, he had castrated himself. Rejected a second time, he now lures knights to their destruction in his garden of bliss, peopled with desirable maidens. His goal is the capture of the Grail itself. Amfortas, in agony and contrition, had prayed fervently before the Grail for a sign of deliverance. Heaven answered his prayer with the words: *Enlightened through compassion, the Innocent Fool. Wait for him, the chosen one.*

Gurnemanz's narration is interrupted by cries from the direction of the lake, and a wild swan flutters to the ground with an arrow in its breast. It has been shot by the thoughtless youth Parsifal, who is dragged before Gurnemanz to account for his action. The boy is so moved by the knight's criticism that he breaks his bow and flings away his arrows. He is unable to say much about his origins, and Gurnemanz declares him to be the dullest person he has ever met – save Kundry. Parsifal tells of his upbringing in the forest with his widowed mother Herzeleide, and his brief encounter with a glittering band of knights who laughed at him and rode away. He had wandered alone, suffering numerous hardships and dangers. At this point, Kundry interjects to tell him abruptly that his mother is now dead. Parsifal is shocked by this news, attacks Kundry and has to be restrained. He nearly faints and, in a gesture of compassion, Kundry fetches water for him from a spring.

The king and his retinue return to the castle. Gurnemanz offers to lead Parsifal to the Grail which, he says, will give him food and drink if he is pure. Gurnemanz has begun to suspect that Parsifal might be the chosen one, the pure fool for whom Amfortas is waiting. The old knight and the foolish boy begin to pass mysteriously from the forest through a rocky wall and finally into the mighty hall of the Grail, although they hardly seem to be moving at all. In the mystical realm of the Grail, 'time becomes space'.

In the hall of the Grail, Parsifal witnesses amazing things – the pleading of the ancient Titurel for the Grail to be unveiled in order to prolong his life, the unbearable suffering of Amfortas when it is at last uncovered, and the sharing of a 'meal of love' of bread and wine by the knights. Despite all these wonders, Parsifal stands stiffly and apparently without emotion, ignoring an invitation to join in the meal. Gurnemanz concludes that he has been mistaken about the boy, and gives up in despair. He calls him a fool and a goose, pushes him outside and slams the door behind him. Softly, a voice intones the mystical words that had been given to Amfortas: 'Enlightened through compassion, the Innocent Fool'; and softly, other voices reply: 'Blessed in faith'.

Act Two

In Klingsor's magic castle, the sorcerer sits surrounded by his instruments of magic and necromancy. He summons the enslaved Kundry to do his bidding, luring knights to their destruction. He refers to her former incarnations as the biblical Herodias and the Norse Gundryggia. She longs for sleep, death and peace but is told that 'only he that defies you will set you free'. In a metallic mirror, his window on the world, Klingsor sees the naïve youth Parsifal approaching. Kundry is instructed to work her wiles on him. Parsifal overcomes Klingsor's warriors who block his way, and a reluctant Kundry prepares to do the magician's will.

The magician and his tower sink rapidly from sight, and in their place rises a magic garden. Lovely, flower-like maidens rush in from all directions and throw themselves at Parsifal, inviting him to play with them. Then Kundry's voice is heard, calling Parsifal by his name – a name he has not heard since his mother used it 'in a dream' long ago. The Flower Maidens disappear and Kundry is seen in a new, alluring form, lying on a couch of flowers. The seduction of Parsifal begins.

Kundry tells him gently that she has always known him, and she describes the circumstances of his mother's death, waiting in vain for him to return. Parsifal is overcome with remorse and Kundry offers to set things right through love. She gives him 'the last greeting of a mother's blessing' and presses her lips to his. There is a long pause, and then Parsifal suddenly realises the significance of Amfortas' wound. He tears himself violently away, struggling to master his feelings. The temptress tries again. She reveals the reason for her own misery and endless wandering – the fact that, in another life, she had laughed at the Saviour when he was suffering on the cross. His compassionate glance had fallen on her, and now she searches for him again from world to world.

When Parsifal continues to rebuff Kundry, she rushes away, cursing him and calling for help to prevent his escape. Klingsor appears on the battlements with the Holy Spear. He hurls it at Parsifal, but the weapon remains suspended over the youth's head. Parsifal grasps it and swings it in the sign of the cross. The castle collapses as if through an earthquake, and the garden rapidly shrivels to a desert.

Act Three

Some years have passed. It is Good Friday and a pleasant spring morning in a flowery meadow at the forest's edge. Gurnemanz emerges from a simple hut. He has grown old and is dressed more like a hermit than a knight. He looks for the source of a strange groaning that he has heard, and finally discovers Kundry lying on the ground amidst the bushes. Kundry now is neither the wild, distracted creature of Act One, nor the voluptuous siren of Act Two, but displays yet another aspect of her complex character –

that of a Magdalen-like penitent. She demurely arranges her hair and clothing and for the remainder of the Act goes about her menial tasks with scarcely a word.

A stranger approaches wearing black armour with closed visor and carrying a spear. He sits wearily on a grassy mound and removes his helmet. Gurnemanz chastises him for being armed on such a holy day, but then recognises him as the boy who killed the swan; the fool whom he had driven away in anger. He also identifies the Sacred Spear and rejoices that he has lived to witness the day of its return.

Parsifal remembers Gurnemanz, and tells him of his trials and perilous battles, throughout which he has kept the spear undefiled. Amfortas, he learns, now longs only for death, for he can bear his suffering no more. The king refuses to perform the holy office and uncover the Grail. Consequently, the knights are in a pitiful state and leaderless. Many have taken to living in the forest like Gurnemanz. Titurel, deprived of the life-giving support of the Grail, has died – a man like all men.

Parsifal laments his own foolishness and his failure to do anything to prevent the misery that has befallen the knights. Moved by compassion and a realisation that the youth is indeed the one for whom they have been waiting, Gurnemanz and Kundry help him to a spring, where Kundry bathes his feet. Gurnemanz scoops up some water and sprinkles it on Parsifal's head. Kundry pours oil on his feet and dries them with her hair, and the old knight pours the rest of the oil on his head, anointing him as the new Grail King.

Parsifal's first duty is to baptise the kneeling Kundry. He then remarks on the beauty of the meadow, contrasting it with Klingsor's rank garden. Gurnemanz tells him that he is experiencing the magic of Good Friday. By the Saviour's loving sacrifice, humanity had been redeemed and, like a new Garden of Eden, nature too had regained its innocence.

In the distance is heard the sombre pealing of bells, and Gurnemanz leads Parsifal and Kundry through the forest, retracing his steps through the rocky walls and into the hall of the Grail. A procession of knights enters bearing the coffin with Titurel's body, and another procession from the opposite direction bears Amfortas on his litter. They confront each other in the centre of the hall, at the covered shrine of the Grail. This time, the knights of Montsalvat are a community utterly without hope. Titurel's coffin is opened, and at the sight of his corpse all break into a sudden wailing. The knights demand that now, for the last time, Amfortas perform his duty and uncover the Grail. He defies them, courting death and tearing open his bandages, imploring the knights to end his torment by plunging their swords into his body.

Unobserved, Parsifal has been watching these dramatic events. Now he steps into the midst of the knights, stretches out the Holy Spear and touches Amfortas' side with its tip. The wound miraculously closes, and Amfortas is healed and spiritually cleansed. Parsifal holds the spear aloft and the shrine is opened. He kneels before the Grail in prayer and it glows brightly as a white dove swoops down and hovers over Parsifal's head. Amfortas and Gurnemanz kneel in homage and, slowly, Kundry sinks lifeless to the ground. Parsifal offers the blessing of the Grail to the worshipping knights and, high in the dome, voices proclaim a final, heavenly benediction:

'Redemption to the Redeemer!'

Richard Wagner
1813–1883

This is one of the most beautiful

monuments that has ever been

erected to the eternal

glory of music.

CLAUDE DEBUSSY

Parsifal *in Context*

Through each of Wagner's mature works for the stage runs a philosophical thread that can be described as follows. Human beings long for a sense of inner peace and fulfilment but are frustrated in this by their attraction to baser instincts and ambitions. This dilemma and its resolution are themes to be found in all of the music dramas, from *Der fliegende Holländer*, in which the Dutchman finds rest only through the love of Senta, to *Parsifal*, in which Amfortas and Kundry are redeemed through the compassion of the 'innocent fool'. Cosima Wagner recognised this when she wrote in her diary, 'from *Holländer* to *Parsifal* – how long the path and yet how similar the character!'

Parsifal, Richard Wagner's last dramatic work, was completed in January 1882. Like Dante's *The Divine Comedy* and Bunyan's *The Pilgrim's Progress*, it is a parable about the journey of a soul through life's trials and temptations to salvation. The composer's grandson, Wieland, noted that even its scenery is 'nothing but the expression of the changing moods of Parsifal's soul, whose path to salvation it is the director's job to reveal'.

In Bunyan's story we find not characters in a literal sense, but personifications of the hero's own conflicting states of mind – Faith, Lust, Malice, Despair and so on. In Dante, although actual historical personages are depicted as ending up in Hell, Purgatory or Paradise, they are associated with the moral weaknesses or strengths that determined their predicament. Similarly, *Parsifal* is not so much a work of character in the usual, dramatic sense, as one of situation and moral discovery.

Biblical references abound in all three works, but whereas Dante invokes the classical spirit of reason (in the person of the Roman poet Virgil) to assist the process of moral awakening, Wagner uses Buddhist imagery and teachings to much the same end. While Bunyan is concerned with the dangers and horrors of a life without faith, Wagner's focus is on a faith that is illuminated by compassion.

Compassion has seldom been uppermost in the minds of men, especially when religion has been the focus of conflict. In 1099 the first Crusaders captured the Holy City of Jerusalem, massacred its inhabitants and installed the Knights Templar in the al-Aqsa Mosque. By 1187, the Christian armies had themselves been beaten by the armies of Saladin, and their most sacred relic, the Holy Cross, captured. In 1188, in response to a tide of public opinion whipped up by preachers and troubadours, the Kings of France and England and the German Emperor Friedrich I (Barbarossa)[1] 'took the Cross' and launched another Crusade. Would-be crusaders were offered spiritual incentives, including a plenary indulgence that St Bernard of Clairvaux explained in the following terms.

> O mighty soldier, O man of war, you now have a cause for which you can fight without endangering your soul; a cause in which to win is glorious and for which to die is but gain. Or are you a shrewd businessman, a man quick to see the profits of this world? If you are, I can offer you a splendid bargain. Do not miss this opportunity. Take the sign of the cross. At once you will have indulgence for all the sins which you confess with a contrite heart. It does not cost you much to buy and if you wear it with humility you will find that it is worth the kingdom of heaven.

---

[1] In his revolutionary years, Wagner had sketched a five-act drama about Friedrich Barbarossa, who had drowned in Asia Minor during the Crusade but who would, according to legend, return in the hour of Germany's need and save his people.

For those who accepted this attractive offer, there were worldly incentives too. Payment of debts was postponed until their return, and their property was taken under the protection of the Church.

One Muslim writer of the time observed that preachers used visual aids to strengthen their exhortations. The writer noted that, among other things, churchmen made a picture showing the Messiah with an Arab striking him and blood on the face of Christ, and they said to the crowds: 'This is the Messiah, struck by Mahomet the prophet of the Muslims, who has wounded and killed Him.' Such hysterical anti-Islamic sentiment coincided with a resurgence of anti-Jewish rioting and violent anti-Semitism in England, France and Germany. Loot taken from the Jews, who were easy targets, enabled many a poor but pious man to join the Crusade.

Of course, cruelty was not confined to Christians in that cruel age. From the middle of the seventh century, Islam had followed the sword through all of North Africa, into Spain, across the Pyrenees to the very gates of Paris, throughout Persia and into India. From the tenth century onwards, scimitars carved their way through the rich and magnificent Hindu and Buddhist kingdoms of India. The bloodshed and destruction were terrible.

As in our own time and in the great Hellenistic age, there was a cross-fertilisation of cultures, from the West and the East. Established power structures came under strain and beliefs were challenged. In particular, the Papacy – the super-power of Europe – was beginning to fracture. And so, in this atmosphere of aggressive, crusading Christianity and renewed interest in the tumultuous east, Chrétien de Troyes, Robert de Boron, Wolfram von Eschenbach and others wrote their tales of knightly romance.

The various medieval stories of Parsifal (also spelt Parzival, Percyvale, Percivale, Percyvelle, Percevelle, Perceval and Percival) were fertile sources for many of the ideas included in

Wolfram von Eschenbach (c. 1170–c. 1220), Knight and Poet.
Author of *Parzival* and *Titurel*, from the Manessa Codex.

Wagner's music drama. Wolfram von Eschenbach's celebrated Middle High German poem of the early thirteenth century has much in common with Chrétien de Troyes' *Perceval ou li Conte du Graal* ('Perceval, or the Story of the Grail'), written in about 1180. For Chrétien, the Grail was a dish or platter. Wolfram was aware of Chrétien's work but claimed that his source had been the work of one Kyot the Provençal, who might or might not have existed. In turn, Chrétien, who died before completing his poem, maintained that he had relied on material in the possession of Count Philip of Flanders. All of these works had their roots in folk tales of antiquity. The Welsh hero Peredur 'of the long lance' (about whom Wagner read in 1860) is identifiable with Perceval, as is the French Perlesvaus (1191–1212) and Perceforest, the hero of a French prose romance of the fourteenth century. The story of Perceforest (so named because he had killed a magician in an impenetrable forest) is just as eclectic as Wagner's *Parsifal,* in that it combines the legends of Alexander the Great and King Arthur. It tells how Alexander, after his expedition to India, is driven by a storm on to the coast of England and makes one of his followers, Perceforest, the king.

From the early sources we learn of characters called Gornemans (or Gornemant), Anfortas, Cundrie and Clinschor, who, in Wagner's work, become Gurnemanz, Amfortas, Kundry and Klingsor. Titurel's name was unchanged, although Wolfram had made him the grandfather of the wounded Grail King rather than his father. In the medieval accounts, Parzival's mother was Herzeloyde (Herzeleide), and his father Gahmuret (Gamuret). One of his sons by the Lady Condwiramurs is Loherangrin (Lohengrin). Munsalvaesche, Mount Salvagge and Montsalvatsch become Montsalvat.

The twelfth-century Burgundian poet, Robert de Boron, who wrote a romance called *Perceval,* was one of the first to link the Grail stories with Arthurian legend, a connection familiar to readers of Sir Thomas Malory's *Le Morte Darthur*, completed in 1470. In Robert de Boron's *Joseph d'Arimathie* (composed between 1180 and 1199), the Christian significance of the legend was extended by turning Chrétien's dish or platter into the cup used by Christ at the Last Supper. Legend (not the Bible) had it that, after the crucifixion, Joseph of Arimathea bore Christ's body to the tomb, the body was washed and blood flowed, which Joseph caught in the Grail. It is Robert's description of the Grail that Wagner recognised and used in his text.

In another work by Robert, known as the *Prose Perceval*, Perceval is shown the Spear ('the lance with which Christ was wounded on the Cross') and the Grail ('the vessel in which Joseph of Arimathea collected the blood and which is called the Grail'). However, a manuscript in the *Bibliotheque de l'Arsenal* in Paris, called *Romans des la Table ronde*, refers to a rumour 'that the Most Holy Grail, in which Joseph of Arimathea had taken up Christ's blood, and the vessel in which Christ had consecrated his body and blood for the first time, as well as the lance that was thrust into his side', were located in Britain.[1] Then again, a Holy Lance formed part of the German Imperial Regalia for centuries.

Such was the importance of relics to the medieval mind that even objects with the most tenuous link to the Saviour became venerated. Thus, for example, we are told in Robert's *Joseph d'Arimathie* that the son of the Roman emperor was cured of leprosy just by the sight of the veil with which Veronica had wiped the face of Christ. The crusaders believed that they had found (and then lost) the True Cross, and found (and retained) the Spear which had pierced Christ's side – the so-called Spear of Longinus – uncovered at the siege of Antioch in 1098.

[1] For a detailed analysis of the Grail stories see Emma Jung and Marie-Louise von Franz, *The Grail Legend*, translated by Andrea Dykes, Princeton University Press, 2nd edition, 1998, and Joseph Campbell, *The Masks of God: Creative Mythology*, London, Secker and Warburg, 1968.

The success of the siege was attributed to the spear's discovery.

Robert drew much of his material from a mysterious 'great book' *(grant livre)*, which was also the source of at least two other Grail romances written between 1215 (the date of the Fourth Lateran Council) and 1230. The authors of these latter works were probably Cistercian monks, anxious to propagate the dogma of the real presence of Christ's body in the sacrament of the altar. The first of these works is *La Queste del Saint Graal*, which offers a vision (a century before Dante's) of the journey of the Christian soul from temporal life to bliss in the presence of God. The second anonymous romance is *L'Estoire del Saint Graal*, which amplifies the legend of Robert's *Joseph* but still describes the Grail – a symbol of supreme spiritual value – as a dish or bowl, and certainly not a chalice. In these accounts, the principal Grail hero is the chaste youth Galahad.

In the *Queste*, the knights Percival, Galahad and Bors are able, by virtue of their purity, to see a marvellous vision of the Saviour. They partake of his real presence (which, in Malory's translation, 'they thought ... so sweet that it was marvellous to tell') and receive the Grail from his hands. In this account, it is the immaculately pure Galahad who heals the Maimed King, with blood flowing from the tip of a spear given to him for that purpose by Christ himself.

Wolfram too wrote of a spear performing a healing function, but it was not a permanent healing, just a temporary one. In his *Parzival* we read of a bleeding spear being held to a wound which Anfortas had received (in the testicles) from the poisoned lance of a heathen adversary. His condition is reflected in his name 'Anfortas', which comes from the old French *Enfertez (Enfermetez)* meaning 'infirmity'. At the time of this wounding, Anfortas, whose battle cry was 'Amor', was jousting for the love of the beautiful Orgeluse. In Wolfram, there is no suggestion that the heathen's weapon was the Spear of Longinus or that the King, at the time, had been doing anything but jousting. The heathen was then killed; a fate not shared by Klingsor for some time, in Wagner's version. Anfortas was 'borne, through God's help, to the Grail: but when he looked upon it his torture only increased, for he now was unable to die'. Wagner followed this point faithfully. However, when the point of the bleeding spear was laid on the wound it drew out the poison and relieved the pain in his body, which hardened to glass around the spear, like ice. In the oldest extant account of the Maimed King – Chrétien's *Perceval,* written about 1180 – we are told that the wound had been inflicted by a javelin thrust through both thighs. This caused such continuing pain that he could not mount a horse, nor walk nor stand. He could only recline on a couch or litter, which is how we find him in Wagner's *Parsifal.*

In Amfortas, Wagner recognised his wounded Tristan, heightened, he said, to a 'state of inconceivable intensification'.[1] Wagner deliberately rejected Wolfram's solution for permanently healing the King, namely that Parzival should ask of Anfortas the question 'Uncle, what ail's thee?' The composer considered this nonsensical.

Wagner did not follow Wolfram or any other source slavishly, but it will be clear by now that many incidents, images and characters in *Parsifal* have their origins in the poems and romances of the Middle Ages. For Wolfram, the Grail was a stone that had fallen from heaven (meteoric perhaps?) and produced an abundance of the most delectable foods. He tells us that the Knights of the Grail 'live from a stone of the purest kind. If you do not know it, it shall be named to you. It is called *lapsit exillis*. This stone is also known as the Grail'. Moreover, says Wolfram, 'there never was a man so ill that, if he saw that stone, would not live, unable to die within a week of that day. Nor in complexion

[1] At one stage, when writing *Tristan und Isolde,* he had even planned to have Parsifal visit Tristan on his sick-bed.

would he ever change. One's appearance, whether maid or man, remains the same as on the day that stone is seen, or as at the start of the years of one's prime. And should one look upon that stone for two hundred years, nothing but one's hair would turn grey'. Wolfram repeats the belief that the stone (which could make the phoenix rise from its ashes) was left behind on earth and guarded by those angels who had remained neutral during the strife between God and Satan.

The basic idea of the stone probably originated with Arabic or Sabean astrology and alchemy, since *lapsit exillis* is also the name of the alchemists' stone. According to Wolfram, the Grail (stone) was discovered by a certain Flegetanis, a pagan natural scientist who read about it in the stars.

In *La Queste del Saint Graal*, the less-than-pure Lancelot tries to approach the Grail (in the form of a dish), but is scorched by a hot wind from it, loses his sight, hearing and power of speech and falls to the ground as if dead. He lies for twenty-four days and nights without speaking, unable to move. Such is the terrible power of the Grail. Other accounts claim that it fills the air with a delightful fragrance, and fills tables 'with sweetmeats that never knights tasted'. Wagner's Parsifal is told that, if his heart is pure, the Grail will give him food and drink.

In many details, Wagner's music drama follows the spirit (and often the letter) of these works of knightly romance. If sometimes we wonder why an aspect of the story takes this turn or that, it is often sufficient to look no further than the medieval sources. Wagner selects, combines and shapes the various elements for his own purposes, just as the ancient poets themselves did. Ultimately, though, it is not the carefully crafted narrative so much as its musical expression that truly reveals the hand of a master at work.

Parsifal is Wagner's most subtle and beautiful score. Ever since its first performance in July 1882, audiences, critics and musicians alike have struggled for words to describe it: 'exquisitely refined', 'lingering sensuousness', 'impressionistic', 'floating', 'dissolving', 'weightless', 'spacious', 'gossamer', 'aloof', the list goes on. Debussy, in a famous phrase, spoke of 'that orchestral colour which seems lit from behind, of which there are such wonderful examples in *Parsifal*'. Wagner himself took infinite pains to create exactly the musical and emotional atmosphere that his vision demanded. Cosima observed in January 1878 that 'just like the imperceptible change and the unfelt development within Parsifal himself, this music develops, changes, hovers – one is wrapped up and borne along by it as if by magic; light gives way to dark as in the colours of clouds at sunset, and all one feels is a constant, unchanging sense of spiritual well-being as one is borne along by it.'

The scaling of the combined musical, dramatic and psychological heights attained in *Götterdämmerung* was, as Brian Magee puts it, an unrepeatable achievement.[1] Magee notes that *Parsifal* demanded, and received, a very different approach. Its sound is highly distinctive and essentially orchestral, and from it were soon to emerge the great adagios in the late symphonies of Bruckner, and the symphonies of Mahler, not to mention important aspects of the music of Richard Strauss, Debussy and later composers. After attending his first performance of *Parsifal* in 1882, Mahler said that he knew that 'this experience, hallowed and unsullied, would stay with me for the rest of my life'.

Significantly, all but one of the main musical themes in *Parsifal* (which are handled very differently from the short, flexible leitmotivs of the *Ring*) originate in the orchestra. The single theme that does not do so is that associated with the foretelling of one who is 'enlightened through compassion, the Innocent Fool' *(durch Mitleid wissend, der reine Tor)*. The music of *Parsifal* unfolds

[1] Brian Magee, *The Philosophy of Schopenhauer*, Oxford University Press, 1983.

in an inevitable, resigned, 'undriven' way, establishing its own relationships of time and space. It too is something of a miracle.

Wagner was particularly attentive to the texture of his orchestral fabric, concerned that its diaphanous, mystical qualities should not become heavy and impenetrable. He was inclined to think, in later years, that he had orchestrated too heavily in *Tristan*. With *Parsifal*, he knew exactly the effect he wanted and how to achieve it. It would be completely different from the *Ring* he said, 'no figurations of that kind; it would be like cloud layers, dispersing and then forming again'. The result is a marvel of transparency and balance.

Wagner's life-long interest in philosophical questions led him to the writings of Rousseau, Kant, Hegel, Feuerbach and, especially, Arthur Schopenhauer, whose ideas had much in common with Buddhism and Brahmanism. Wagner first encountered Schopenhauer in September 1854 when working on *Die Walküre*. In his autobiography he tells us that he read *The World as Will and Representation*, Schopenhauer's *magnum opus*, four times in quick succession. He describes it as a work that became vastly important to him. This encounter with Schopenhauer's writings was, in fact, the single most important intellectual event in his life, and significantly influenced his artistic direction. He came to regard 'Schopenhauerian philosophy and *Parsifal* as the crowning achievement!'

In the years after 1854, he also read Buddhist and Brahmanic material, notably Burnouf's *Introduction à l'histoire du bouddhisme indien*, Adolf Holtzmann's *Indische Sagen* (Indian Legends), F. Köppen's *Die Religion des Buddha und ihre Entstehung* (The Buddhist Religion and Its Origin) 2 volumes, 1857–59, Christian Lassen's *Indische Altertumskunde* (Study of Ancient Indian Civilisation), in 4 volumes, 1844–61, Colebrookes's *Essay on the Vedas*, the *Ramayana*, the *Upanishads* and the *Bhagavadgita*.

In May 1856 Wagner drafted a sketch for a music drama to

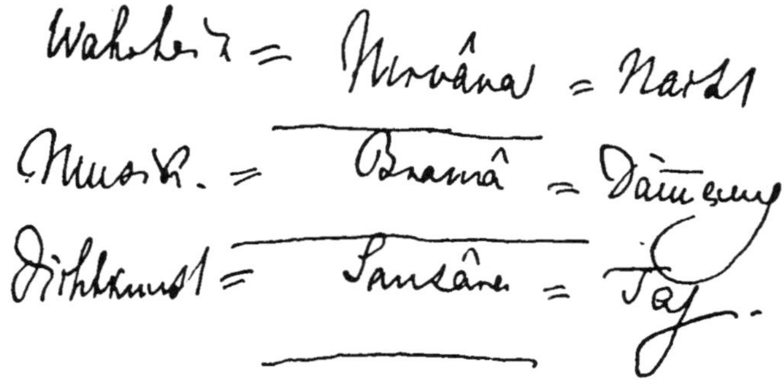

Wagner's own entry of May 1868 in his diary, the 'Brown Book', linking Buddhist concepts with dramatic imagery and modes of expression. His words mean:

Truth = *Nirvana* = Night
Music = *Brahma* = Twilight
Poetry = *Samsara* = Day.

Nirvana is the 'blowing out' of the fires of greed, hatred and delusion; the extinction of self. Wagner also likened it to 'untroubled, pure harmony'. *Brahma* is the world soul (and the chief God of Brahmanism). *Samsara* is the restlessness of a worldly life; the agitation of selfishness.

be called *Die Sieger* (The Victors). The title was inspired by the Jinas, Indian holy men whose name in Sanskrit means 'victors'. Their victory was over human passions. *Die Sieger* dealt with an event in the legendary life of the Buddha, one of whose titles was Jina – the Victor. Wagner himself described the sketch as being based on a simple legend of a low-caste maiden (called Prakriti) who is received into a pious order of mendicants 'as a result of her painfully intense and purified love for Ananda, the chief disciple of the Buddha'. Wagner was especially attracted to the story's secondary theme of reincarnation as a vehicle for his compositional technique of Emotional Reminiscence, usually referred to by the term 'leitmotiv'. 'Only music' he said, 'can convey the mysteries of reincarnation.' *Die Sieger* was never developed beyond a sketch but some of its ideas were used again in *Parsifal*, and Prakriti reappeared (transformed) as Kundry.

Wagner's fascination with Buddhism intensified as the years went by and coloured his general philosophy. It is seen most vividly in *Parsifal* and in *Tristan und Isolde* (where, for example, one finds a correlation between Truth, Nirvana and Night) but there are also traces in *Der Ring des Nibelungen*. In 1856, the same year as *Die Sieger*, Wagner drafted a Buddhist ending for the *Ring*, with Brünnhilde achieving enlightenment (that is, becoming a Buddha herself) and attaining Nirvana. That ending was subsequently replaced by the present one.

Cosima Wagner, in her diary entry for Saturday, 20 July 1878, wrote 'When I was looking through some papers with him yesterday, I came upon the original theme for *Sangst du nicht, dein Wissen*; I tell Richard that the present theme (meant at first for the Buddha) pleases me far more.' What is this theme that was composed originally for the Buddha in *Die Sieger*? It is used by Siegfried when he tells Brünnhilde, 'You said that all your wisdom came by the light of your love to me'. In Wotan's final scene with Erda, it is used to express his wisdom in accepting the inevitability of change and his own demise. Although the theme is usually referred to as 'the world's inheritance', it should more properly be thought of as 'the getting of wisdom' or 'enlightenment'; hence the connection in Wagner's mind with that defining characteristic of the Buddha. In *Parsifal,* the concept is taken further, for it is not just enlightenment but 'enlightenment through compassion' that is the motivating force of this work, and the consolation that it offers to a suffering humanity.

As with most of his ideas, Wagner's thoughts on religion were far from conventional. He was anti-clerical in general, and anti-Catholic and anti-Jewish in particular. By temperament he was non-conformist and by conviction an individualist. Institutionalised, hierarchical, communal religion was anathema to him. Nevertheless, he told Cosima

> This need for religion shows that human beings are in fact disposed towards good. What a comforting example, after all, is offered by such a religion as that of Buddha, in which the reward is the gentle heart itself and the punishment the angry heart!

However, he could also say that 'the absence of all ideality brings the soul blissful peace, and the way to this peace is through Jesus Christ'; and, on another occasion that, for him, the whole of Christianity is contained in Holy Communion. Cosima also confided to her diary: 'Over our breakfast together, he talks about the book on the Buddha and says that by giving much attention to the Buddha one learns to understand Christianity.'

Why was the Buddhist opera *Die Sieger* never finished? The answer is, again, to be found in Cosima's Diaries. In her entry for 7 May 1878, she noted that the sweet fragrance of the Indian Sagarika prompted him to say that the reason he would never carry out his Indian project was that he did not know the names of the flowers, and these were an integral part of the subject. On 27 September 1882 (that is, less than five months before

Wagner's death) she wrote: 'We now talk almost constantly about the Buddha; recently Richard remarked how impossible it would have been for him to set him to music if he had had to concern himself with mango trees, lotus blossoms, etc'. He had also told her on an earlier occasion: 'My difficulty there (with *Die Sieger*) is the locality and the speech. Christianity is all noble simplicity, but in Buddhism there is so much learning, and learning is very inartistic'. In other words, he had wanted a narrative framework with more familiar (European and Christian) imagery.

In 1857, while he was wrestling with the problems of his Buddhist story of renunciation and compassion, Wagner was moved by a beautiful spring day on the Wesendonck estate near Zürich, where he and his first wife, Minna, had temporarily made their home. He associated that tranquil scene of reawakened nature with the world's new 'beginning', achieved through Christ's sacrifice on the cross. His mind went back to a time twelve years earlier when, during a rest cure at Marienbad, he had first read Wolfram's *Parzival*. Various ideas began to mingle in his mind and, in April that year, just eleven months after the sketch for *Die Sieger*, Wagner completed the first prose sketch of *Parsifal*. A gestation period of twenty-five years then followed, with the work only achieving its final form in January 1882.

For many years, Wagner spoke of completing *Die Sieger* in old age, after he had finished *Parsifal*. The two works were linked in his mind, and his affection for the Buddhist story was strong. *Die Sieger*, he thought, would be 'gentler' than *Parsifal* and (unlike the Grail stories) involve fewer references to blood. However, by April 1882 a sense of realism and a feeling of exhaustion caused him to abandon these ideas for good. He concluded that *Parsifal* ought certainly to be his final work since, in the Knights of the Grail, he had given full expression to his ideas of a community. *Die Sieger*, he said, could only repeat these ideas 'in a weak and insignificant way'.

The blending of Christian legends and sacraments with Buddhist legends and teachings is an extraordinary idea, but Wagner saw no conflict in this at all. There are, after all, many common elements in Christian and Buddhist practice, if not theology. The Buddha, for example, taught: 'Let a person overcome anger by love, overcome evil by good, overcome the greedy by liberality, the liar by truth.' He also taught that 'The fault of others is easily noticed, but that of oneself is difficult to perceive', and again that 'The perfect man is nothing unless he pours out kindness on his fellow creatures, unless he consoles the abandoned.' Such teachings would hardly be out of place in the Gospels.

In a letter to Liszt of 1855, Wagner cited contemporary research which suggested that Buddhist ideas had flowed westwards after the extension of Alexander's empire to the Indus in 327 BC, and had influenced Christian doctrine. Schopenhauer himself had written, rather condescendingly, 'I cannot give up the belief that the doctrines of Christianity can in some way be derived from these primitive religions.' The evidence (such as it is) is entirely circumstantial, but it is intriguing to speculate that the wise men from the east might have brought more than gold, frankincense and myrrh to Roman Judea! The most that one can say is that Buddhism began its great peregrinations throughout India and into South East Asia and Persia between the third and first centuries BC, and that the earliest contact between Buddhism and the classical world occurred around the beginning of the third century BC.

Schopenhauer had also sought to distinguish 'authentic' Christianity from 'the relics of Old Testament mythology and the accretion of misguided dogma with which it is encumbered'; a theme to which Wagner returned in some of his more fanciful writings in his last years.

Throughout his life, Wagner pondered on religion and its

place in human society. Friedrich Nietzsche, who at first idolised Wagner and then dramatically fell out with him for a complex mixture of reasons, regarded *Parsifal* as a betrayal, a work of Counter-Reformation in more senses than one. In January 1878, Wagner had sent him the text of *Parsifal*, inscribed (as he thought, to a friend) with his typically jocular sense of irony: 'Cordial greetings and best wishes to his dear friend Friedrich Nietzsche, from Richard Wagner (Supreme Councillor of the Church – for the information of Professor Overbeck).' The reference to Overbeck was an in-joke, intended to stress the *unecclesiastical* nature of the text.[1] However, Nietzsche was already forming a very different opinion of Wagner, and found in *Parsifal* further justification for his *volte-face*.

Nietzsche, the brilliant, violently anti-Christian son of a protestant clergyman, maintained that 'What you hear is Rome – Rome's faith without the text'. In his view 'Richard Wagner, apparently the greatest victor, actually a now decayed and confused decadent, sank suddenly down, helpless and in pieces, before the Christian Cross'; Christianity had been transformed into theatre; the work was 'knee-bending before Romantic Catholicism'; the heroic Siegfried had been replaced with the self-denying Parsifal. He described the work as 'an apostasy and reversion to sickly Christian obscurantist ideals'. 'Can it be,' wrote Nietzsche, 'that a hatred of life has got the better of him, as it got the better of Flaubert? For *Parsifal* is a work of malice and revenge, a secret poison against the preconditions of life, a wicked work. The sermon of chastity is an incitement to pathology, and I would despise anyone who did not feel in *Parsifal* an attack upon morality itself.'[2] Wagner was genuinely shocked by Nietzsche's attacks, and could not fathom their motivation. Cosima was

1 Franz Overbeck, Protestant theologian, Professor at Basel and a friend of Nietzsche, had written a book about the non-Christian nature of modern theology.

2 Nietzsche, *Wagner as the Apostle of Chastity*. Nietzsche attacked Wagner in many other essays and books (some are listed in Further Reading, page 130).

equally wounded by his description of her as a voluntary sacrificial animal!

Nietzsche, for all his intimacy with the Wagner household during the eight years between 1868 and 1876, failed to understand what really made Wagner the artist 'tick'. Most of all, he failed to see that Wagner's mind was forever restless and could not be contained. Nietzsche recalled 'how enthusiastically Wagner walked, in his time, in the footsteps of the philosopher Feuerbach. Feuerbach's theme of "healthy sensuality"! In the thirties and forties of this century, that had sounded to Wagner, as to many Germans – they called themselves the young Germans – like the Gospel of Redemption. Has he now finally unlearned that song?' Well, yes he had. He had begun to do so ever since he encountered Schopenhauer, whom Nietzsche, with his theories of the morally self-determined man and the *Übermensch* (uninhibited human being) came to reject. Wagner was later to observe, 'everything depends on facing the truth, even if it is unpleasant. What about myself in relation to Schopenhauer's philosophy – when I was completely Greek, an optimist? But I made the difficult admission, and from this act of resignation emerged ten times stronger.' Nietzsche regarded Schopenhauer and Wagner (and *Parsifal*) as denying the 'will' in favour of concepts such as morality, whereas he rejected such notions. He not only asserted individual 'will' but also advocated its *unqualified* assertion. Nietzsche was, in his own view, saying *Yes* to life, while Wagner in *Parsifal* was saying *No* to life.

In the 1930s, the Nazi Party also found *Parsifal* unpalatable – even 'ideologically unacceptable' – and played down its religious and compassionate central themes in favour of something called 'blood mysticism', and then banned performances altogether (including at Bayreuth) after 1939.[1] Perhaps they were also

---

[1] See Frederic Spotts, *Bayreuth. A History of the Wagner Festival*, Yale University Press, 1994.

aware that the composer himself had remarked in 1877 'I am writing *Parsifal* only for my wife – if I had to depend on the German spirit, I should have nothing more to say.'

The relationship between Wagner and Nietzsche had probably been doomed from the beginning, despite its heady moments, and their views grew further and further apart after 1876. However, there were also less philosophical aggravations. Nietzsche was pre-eminently a philosopher who thought he was also a composer. He was a good pianist and proud of his seventy or so compositions, many of which he performed for the Wagners and their friends. The works are palely reminiscent of Schumann and Mendelssohn, with occasional forays into Lisztian harmonies. Michael Tanner, in his comments on possible reasons for the rift between the two men, says:

> Not to be discounted are Nietzsche's own ambitions as a composer, the most embarrassing of his failures. A man who could play his own amateur piano pieces to Wagner, and who could continue to write, until much later, choral pieces that sound like Congregational Church hymns with a few wrong notes but are called *Hymn to Life* or *Hymn to Friendship* was evidently not able to judge his own gifts in this respect.[1]

Wagner regarded Nietzsche as a friend and was restrained in his criticism, but Hans von Bülow, who had been a pupil of Liszt, felt no such qualms and asked the would-be composer: 'Can't you think of a better way to kill me?'

Considering the vehemence of Nietzsche's attacks on Wagner during his lifetime, it comes as a surprise to find that, five years after the composer's death, he could write of the 'enchantment which this incomparable man has exercised over me ... I loved and honoured Richard Wagner more than anyone else, him, the

[1] Michael Tanner, *Nietzsche*, Oxford University Press, 1994.

most profound and most daring, also the most misunderstood of all those who are hard to understand today.'[1]

Parsifal was completed towards the end of Wagner's life, but in it we see the working out of musical and dramatic ideas that are as breath-taking and original as any that Wagner conceived. These ideas had been evolving since the 1840s and '50s – those seminal years to which all of his mature works can ultimately be traced. He commented to Cosima in January 1882, 'I was telling myself today that it is quite remarkable that I held this work back for my fullest maturity; I know what I know and what is in it; and the new school ... can take their lead from it.'

One of the most demanding projects in Wagner's later years was the creation of the festival performances at Bayreuth. The design and construction of the Festspielhaus, the selection and training of singers and orchestral players from all over Germany, the raising of funds and the mounting of the first *Ring* production in 1876 (which he supervised in every respect) was a superhuman task with few parallels in the history of art. It consumed vast amounts of energy. Afterwards, when he was depressed and struggling to meet the debts incurred by the first Festival, Wagner looked back at the Bayreuth experiment with a mixture of amazement and despair, and concluded that it had been a monumental folly. However, he had created a new type of theatrical experience which required a special kind of performance, and an audience who took that performance seriously. To these ends he had adopted the design of the ancient Greek amphitheatre with its egalitarian seating and perfect sight lines, a darkened auditorium which focussed attention on the stage, a double proscenium which heightened the sense of illusion, and a sunken orchestra pit which blended the sound and removed the visual distraction of conductor and players. Everything was designed to present the

[1] An unpublished note written in conjunction with *The Case of Wagner* 1888. Quoted in *The Richard Wagner Museum, Bayreuth*, 8th edition, 1997, M. Eger and S. Friedrich.

Ring in ideal conditions. The Festival Theatre is therefore truly a child of *Der Ring des Nibelungen*.

Parsifal, on the other hand, was composed with the unique qualities of the theatre in mind. The composer knew exactly how the sound would bloom in the remarkable auditorium, with its sunken orchestra pit and superb acoustics, and he was confident that his designers and technicians would do justice to the transformations and other dazzling scenic effects. This time (in contrast to 1876) his expectations were almost completely realised. The performances were as near to ideal as anyone could have imagined, and the Festival actually made a profit. Sixteen performances of *Parsifal* were given in 1882 (it was the only work performed), and it constituted the entire Festival again in 1883 and 1884. Even the sharp-tongued critic Eduard Hanslick fell silent.

Amongst the visitors who attended the first performance of *Parsifal* at Bayreuth was the New York music critic and, subsequently, author of *The Complete Opera Book*, Gustave Kobbé. Of that historic event he wrote:

> I saw Wagner several times in the summer of 1882. Except that his hair was grey, the description [in the 1849 warrant for his arrest for revolutionary activities] still held good, especially as regards his rapidity of movement and speech, to which I may add a marked vivacity of gesture. There, too, I saw the friend, who had helped him over so many rough places in his early career, Franz Liszt, his hair white with age, but framing a face as strong and keen as an eagle's. I saw them seated at a banquet, and with them Cosima, Liszt's daughter, who was Wagner's second wife, and their son, Siegfried Wagner; Cosima the image of her father, and Siegfried a miniature replica of the composer to whom we owe *Lohengrin* and the music-dramas that followed it. The following summer one of the four was missing. I have the *Parsifal* programme with mourning border signifying that the performances of the work were in memory of its creator.[1]

[1] Gustave Kobbé, *Kobbé's Complete Opera Book*, editied and revised by the Earl of Harewood. Putnam and Company, 8th edition, London 1969.

Parsifal was more than just a theatrical experience; it was also Wagner's *credo*, the product of a lifetime's reading and reflection. Little wonder then that he called it *A Festival Play for the Dedication of the Stage*, and was reluctant to let other theatres get their hands on it. More pragmatically, the experience of seeing fragments of the *Ring* being played all over the place, with performances manipulated (in Cosima's hypersensitive terms) 'to denigrate the Festival performances ... [and] make fun of its author' had led to a nervousness about sanctioning productions over which the author had no control. The possibility that *Parsifal* might suffer a similar fate did not bear thinking about. In November 1882 Cosima confided to her diary, 'In the afternoon he thinks of Bayreuth and says it would probably be a good thing if he were to stage all his works there, and they should also be staged there after his death, for they still survive [*sic*], and the way in which they are done elsewhere is appalling.'

The law relating to copyright and royalties within the German states prior to unification was chaotic. It went unregularised until 1870 and, even then, was nowhere near as comprehensive as the modern law on the subject. Of course, occasionally the chaos worked in Wagner's favour, enabling him to 'sell' the ownership of the *Ring* scores to both Otto Wesendonck (in Switzerland) and King Ludwig II (in Bavaria) on separate occasions. After the inaugural 1876 Festival, financial pressures had made the sale of the *Ring*'s performance rights unavoidable, although Wagner had resisted this for as long as he could. Even the ownership of the exquisite and intimate *Siegfried Idyll*, written to mark Cosima's thirty-third birthday and the birth of their son, had to be sold in 1877 to make ends meet. Cosima wept bitter tears over this. However, *Parsifal* was a different matter. The 1882 season had produced a profit of 135,000 marks and, literally, for the first time in Wagner's life there was no need to sell his creations to raise money. He could enjoy the luxury of retaining complete artistic control for as long as he wished.

It comes as a surprise therefore, to discover that, in the late 1870s and in 1880, during emotional low points, and in despair of Germany and its governments, Wagner had seriously contemplated moving to America (Minnesota to be precise) to establish a stage school and to give there the first performance of *Parsifal*. This work, he said, would be dedicated to the American nation, and he would not allow performances to be given anywhere else (e.g. Bayreuth) until then. King Ludwig was horrified. 'Your roses will not grow on America's sterile soil', wrote the King, 'where selfishness, lovelessness and Mammon hold sway'. Ultimately, the American dream came to nothing, not least because it would have involved a capital endowment by the Americans of one million dollars, which failed to materialise.

Wagner decided to stay put and wrote to the King in September 1880: 'I must say it again and again that handing over this work to our municipal theatre audiences, with their late comers, early leavers, with their banging of seats and air of boredom, would be as sinful as the desecration of the Eleusinian mysteries'. Ludwig agreed. He also agreed to release Wagner from a promise made in the desperate days of 1878 to allow the Munich Opera to perform the work following its Bayreuth premiere. And so, the Bayreuth festival theatre was 'dedicated' by the first performance of *Parsifal* on 26 July 1882.

In his *Reminiscences of Richard Wagner*, the theatre producer Angelo Neumann maintained that, in August 1882, Wagner had promised him the exclusive rights to produce *Parsifal* anywhere in the world, except Bayreuth. Neumann was already touring with the *Ring*, for which he had now secured use of the original Bayreuth sets. But, said Neumann, Wagner changed his mind on *Parsifal* and asked to be released from this promise on the understanding that Neumann would indeed be granted exclusive rights – eventually. He could hardly have done otherwise, given the king's readiness to forego a Munich production on the grounds put to him in 1880.

Nevertheless, in 1881, when the Wagners had been holidaying in Palermo, Cosima recorded in her diary that Richard had told her he intended to sell *Haus Wahnfried* (the family home in Bayreuth paid for by King Ludwig), hand over the performances of *Parsifal* to Neumann and settle down in Italy. He was, she said, tired and run down. By August 1882, notwithstanding the Festival's success, Wagner was still in a very anti-Bayreuth mood and again spoke of handing over *Parsifal* and the festival theatre to Neumann. However, a few weeks later, Cosima wrote that he was angry when Neumann asked for the performing rights to *Parsifal*. We shall never know for certain what Wagner's long-term intentions were, for within six months he was dead and his inconsolable widow could not bring herself to sell the performing rights to anyone. Wagner did not leave a will.

In 1884 and again in 1885, the Bayreuth production of *Parsifal* was staged privately at the Court Theatre in Munich for an increasingly eccentric Ludwig II, without whom, it must be said, there would have been no Bayreuth theatre and probably no *Parsifal*. Ludwig had declined to attend the premiere on grounds of poor health, much to Wagner's distress. The embargo against other productions held until 1903. In that year, the Metropolitan Opera in New York, unfettered by international copyright obligations, mounted a production of its own, with great success. The German copyright restriction finally expired in 1913, thirty years after the composer's death, and despite Cosima's strenuous efforts to persuade the *Reichstag* to extend it.

The 'illegal' New York performances provoked sanctimonious outrage amongst the Bayreuth faithful (and German opera directors, who were furious that they would have to wait another ten years). The phrase 'rape of the Grail' was heard. The Mayor of New York and certain clerics there thought the work blasphemous and were inclined to support a ban. However, the performances went ahead and they made a tremendous impact. In just two years, no fewer than 354 performances of *Parsifal* were given around the United States.

Dame Nellie Melba attended a New York performance several years later and recorded the experience in her memoirs. The performance had begun at eleven o'clock in the morning, Melba recalled. She had been given a box and felt obliged to attend, but she was very tired, having sung in *Traviata* the night before. She was in no mood for such a long work, and really wished she were somewhere else. Then came the music.

> I cannot explain quite what happened to me during the unforgettable act that followed [she wrote]. One cannot crystallise these things in prose ... The theatre ceased to exist, I ceased to exist – I was a disembodied spirit, floating in realms of pure music. But I do remember that at the end of the act, when the curtain fell, and the house remained wrapped in silence – I put my hand up to my head and felt that I had a hat on. A hat? What was a hat? It seemed something unreal, grotesque. And then Ada Sassoli, that great little harpist, sitting by me, said something which made me realise I was on earth. She took my hand, and at the touch of the warm, human contact, I leant back in my chair and sobbed ... The next thing I remember is that I was being led out by my friends, and walked up and down the snow-covered pavements, for a quarter of an hour. All the time I felt gradually that I was returning to earth. But from where? To what strange sphere had that music transported me? I suppose that I shall never know. But I do know that the coming back was infinitely painful, and that when I afterwards found myself forced to go out to lunch, the tinkling of the little orchestra in the restaurant was so torturing that unless I had asked them to stop I believed I should have gone mad.[1]

[1] Melba, Nellie, *Melodies and Memories*, Hamish Hamilton, London, 1925. Annotated by John Cargher, 1980, p. 174.

Unlike the United States, Melba's native land of Australia was bound by the Berne Copyright Convention to observe the embargo, but local curiosity was intense and prompted at least one oddity. In December 1906, the impresario J.C. Williamson staged in Sydney what was described as 'an entirely Australian drama, *Parsifal* – written by the Reverend Hillhouse Taylor and following the Wagnerian story in spirit'. The role of Kundry was played by the American actress Miss Minnie Tittell Brune. Amongst the other characters were some who cannot be found in Wagner's work, such as 'Maidens of the Holy Grail', 'the Dumb Maiden' and 'Zana, Klingsor's slave and companion'. It is said that, in the final act of this unique work, 'amid the flashing of lightning and the roaring of thunder, the heavens caved in and the world imploded, leaving only shattered columns, broken arches, Kundry and Parsifal.'[1] Clearly the Reverend Hillhouse Taylor had, with one stroke, achieved a remarkable synthesis of *Parsifal* and *Götterdämmerung*!

Amongst Wagner's works, *Parsifal* occupies a special place, not only because of its exceptional musical qualities but also because of the feelings that inspired it. Wagner disclosed the very personal nature of his motivation in a memoir written shortly after the first performance. In it he said:

> The effect of the visual and acoustical atmosphere in the theatre ... was to lift us out of the everyday world, and our awareness of this emerged clearly when we felt ourselves being told to return to this world. In truth, *Parsifal* itself owes its conception and its execution to my flight from this very world. Can anyone look with open heart and mind at the deception, the hypocrisy, the organised, legalised theft and murder around us without sometimes being forced to avert one's gaze from the world in horror and disgust? And where then can one look? So often into the abyss of death.

---

[1] Michael and Joan Tallis, *The Silent Showman*, Wakefield Press, Adelaide, 1999.

Even Friedrich Nietzsche came to recognise in *Parsifal* another *Divine Comedy*. He heard its music for the first time four years after Wagner's death and, notwithstanding his earlier denunciations, wrote of 'a sublime, extraordinary feeling and spiritual experience in music at its most fundamental … a synthesis of spiritual states which many, including so-called superior minds, will consider irreconcilable … an intellectual and psychological penetration which cuts through the soul like a knife. The only thing like it is in Dante – nowhere else.'

Nothing in the world

has ever made so overwhelming

an impression on me.

All my innermost heartstrings

throbbed.

JEAN SIBELIUS

Love, Faith and Hope?

The Prelude to *Parsifal* is remarkable for its expressive and mysterious beauty. Wagner called it a 'preface' or 'preamble', likening it to the preamble of a sermon, because the themes are simply stated one after another. It was first performed by the Meiningen orchestra in the salon of *Haus Wahnfried* in Bayreuth on Cosima's birthday, 1878. Two years later another private performance was given, this time for King Ludwig in Munich. Cosima required no assistance in interpreting what she heard, for she had lived with its creation and understood its place in the drama. However, for the king, Wagner drafted an explanatory note in which he described the main ideas of Love, Faith and Hope, and the way in which these interacted with each other.

Wagner explained the Prelude in the rather overwrought terms that he knew would appeal to the highly romantic Ludwig. He understood the king's temperament well, and we too can get some idea of it from a letter of May 1868, in which the king first set out his thoughts for the fantasy castle of *Neuschwanstein*, in the Bavarian alps. The letter ran in part: 'You will know who the guest is whom I want to invite and entertain there. The spot is one of the loveliest that can be found, inviolable and inaccessible, a worthy temple for the godlike Friend [i.e. Wagner] through whom alone can flower the salvation and true blessedness of the world.' The Minstrel's Hall of *Neuschwanstein* would one day be decorated with scenes from the 'life' of Parsifal, including 'portraits' of Parsifal's mother and father. Ludwig was, as his cousin the Empress Elisabeth put it, 'not mad; he was just an eccentric living in a world of dreams.'

For the king, Wagner described the Prelude to *Parsifal* as follows:

'Love – Faith – Hope?'

First theme: 'Love'.

'Take ye My body, take My blood, in token of our love!'
(repeated in faint whispers by angel voices)

'Take ye My blood, My body take, in memory of Me!'
(again repeated in whispers)

Second theme: 'Faith'.

'Promise of redemption through faith. Firmly and stoutly faith declares itself, exalted, willing even in suffering. To the promise renewed Faith answers from the dimmest heights – as on the pinions of a snow-white dove – hovering downwards – usurping more and more the hearts of men, filling the world, the whole world of Nature, with the mightiest force, then glancing up again to heaven's vault as if appeased.

But once more, from out the awe of solitude, throbs forth the cry of loving pity; the agony, the holy sweat of Olivet, the divine death-throes of Golgotha – the body pales, the blood flows forth, and glows now in the chalice with the heavenly glow of blessing, shedding on all that lives and languishes the grace of ransom won by Love. For him who – fearful rue for sin at heart – must quail before the Godlike vision of the Grail, for Amfortas, sinful keeper of the halidom, we are made ready: will redemption heal the gnawing torments of his soul? Once more we hear the promise, and – we hope!'[1]

---

[1] Nineteenth-century translation by William Ashton Ellis.

A more sober analysis might go something like this. The theme of Love, which rises softly and slowly through the opening bars, reminds us of the Saviour who, in the supreme act of love, gave his body and blood to redeem a world gone wrong. Redemption is promised through Faith, which fills human hearts and all creation with the assurance of a new beginning. The Grail (expressed musically by the ancient theme known as the Dresden Amen) focuses our thoughts on the need for salvation. We are reminded of the suffering of Christ and the frailty and suffering of humanity personified by Amfortas. And yet, do we not through faith have reason to hope?

The final idea is expressed as a question, mirrored in the orchestra by a melody which soars upwards over a harmony that remains uncertain. The Prelude comes to an end with the chord of the dominant seventh still unresolved.

When I came out

of the Festspielhaus,

unable to speak a word,

I knew that I had experienced

supreme greatness and

supreme suffering …

GUSTAV MAHLER

The Innocent Fool

Wolfram's poem of *Parzival*, which made such an impression on Wagner, was written between 1200 and 1212. In it the hero's father is identified as Gahmuret of Anjou, supposedly a close relation of King Arthur. In this account, Gahmuret travels eastwards in search of adventure, visiting exotic places such as Baghdad, Persia, Morocco, Damascus and Arabia. While he is on one such adventure, he meets the Moorish Queen Belacane, who bears him a pied black and white son, Feirefiz. Returning to Europe, Gahmuret wins the hand of Queen Herzeloyde (Heart's Sorrow) but soon sets out on another adventure, only to be killed in Baghdad. Shortly after his death, Herzeloyde gives birth to Parzival. So, Parzival (Parsifal), like Tristan and Siegfried, belongs to that company of heroes who have never known their fathers.[1] Wagner's own father died when he was just five months old and, like Parsifal, he too was raised by his mother.

Herzeloyde is determined to prevent her son from following in his father's footsteps to adventure and death. She withdraws to the forest, taking the boy with her and raises him in a state of ignorance of worldly dangers and attractions. This is the origin of his naïveté. By chance, Parzival encounters some knights in the forest. Initially he thinks they are angels and falls to his knees, but they soon put him right and tell him about Arthur's court. He decides to follow them. In Wagner's text, Parsifal mentions his encounter with a glittering band of knights, who just laugh at him and ride on. Herzeloyde realises that she cannot prevent her

---

[1] Tristan and Siegfried also lost their mothers shortly after birth.

son from leaving, but she dresses him in the rough and ready attire of a bumpkin or fool, hoping that he will not be taken seriously and will be sent home. She gives him some parting advice which is relevant to events in the opera: 'Ask advice of those with grey hair', and 'Strive to win a good lady's ring and then to kiss and embrace her'. She has not told him of his heritage or even his name (details which Wagner uses), but has always referred to him as *bon fils, cher fils, beau fils*. Parzival leaves her and, overwhelmed by grief, she falls dead.

Parzival meets his cousin Sigune and learns his real name from her. She tells him that 'Parzival' means 'right through the middle' for, she says, 'a false love has cut its furrow right through your mother's heart'. In fact, the older, French form 'Perceval' is more likely to have meant 'pierces (or penetrates) the valley', implying perhaps that he was destined to penetrate the dark valley of the unconscious.[1] 'Parsifal' certainly does not derive from pseudo-Arabic words *'fal parsi'* meaning 'foolish innocent', which is the explanation given by Kundry to Parsifal in Act Two. Wagner admitted that he had obtained this meaning from Joseph Görres' book *Die christliche Mystik* (Christian Mysticism) which he read with some scepticism. He also admitted to making up the suggestion that the words were derived from an Arabic dialect. He was an indefatigable player of word games (*Die Meistersinger* is full of them), including ironies, puns and anagrams, of which another is Tantris, the disguise adopted by Tristan in Ireland.

In Wolfram's account, Parzival kills the Red Knight, Ither of Gaheviez, with an arrow through the visor, in order to win his bright red armour. Thus Parzival becomes, in appearance at least, the Red Knight. He insists on wearing the armour on top of his fool's garb. He is taught some rudimentary weaponry but his arrows are taken away from him as being unworthy of a knight.

[1] This is the Jungian interpretation given by Emma Jung and Marie-Louise von Franz in *The Grail Legend*.

He subsequently meets the 'grey-haired' Prince Gurnemanz de Graharz and learns from him the basics of chivalry. Gurnemanz is surprised to see that, beneath his armour, Parzival is dressed in fool's garb, although he recognises that his 'form is noble'. Wagner makes use of these details by having the old knight Gurnemanz remark to Parsifal 'You yourself seem eagle-like and nobly born. Why did your mother not let you learn to use better weapons?'

Wolfram's Parzival sets out on adventures, and marries the beautiful Queen Condwiramurs (who will become the mother of Lohengrin). However, he soon leaves his bride in order to look for his mother, being still unaware of her death. He comes to a lake where he meets a richly attired fisherman, called Anfortas.

Wagner used many of the details from Wolfram's poem in the first Act of *Parsifal*, but there are some important differences. There are no references to a brother – pied or otherwise. Parsifal hears his name not from a cousin but from the lips of Kundry, in Act Two. There is no mention of his being married (in fact he appears to be a complete innocent in the matter of female charms – other than maternal ones). Amfortas comes to the lake not to fish but to bathe.[1] The knight Gawan (Gauvain, Gawain) has a major role in earlier accounts, in which he becomes, in a sense, Perceval's double – a kind of shadow brother.[2] In Wolfram, Gawan behaves in a predictable, knightly fashion, whereas Parzival seems more human. It was Gawan who asked of his grandmother, imprisoned in Clinschor's castle 'Dear lady, can you tell me something of Clinschor?' words echoed in Wagner's version by a squire to Gurnemanz: 'But father, speak and tell us plainly; you knew Klingsor – how could that be?'

---

[1] Wolfram's Fisher can be found in a number of legends; in some he is known as the 'Rich Fisher' and in others as the 'Maimed King' or the 'Fisher King'. It has been suggested that he was symbolically 'fishing for Christ', whose sign in early Christian iconography was a fish.

[2] Compare Gunther and Siegfried in *Götterdämmerung*.

Poverty and Humility, signified by two knights riding the same horse.
The Seal of the Poor Knights of Christ and of the Temple of Solomon
(The Knights Templar).

It has been suggested that, originally, Gauvain was the real Grail hero, being supplanted by Perceval when the story was Christianised, just as Perceval was himself later replaced by Galahad. In Wagner's text, Gawan is reduced to a passing reference, from which we learn that the healing herb that he found had failed to alleviate the king's suffering, and that he has sped away to continue his search. He is not mentioned again, but the fact that he is mentioned at all is another reminder of the source material.

Kundry makes her first appearance quite early in the opera. If Brünnhilde is Wagner's most fully developed character, Kundry is his most enigmatic. He was fascinated by her and told Cosima so on more than one occasion. Her character undergoes sudden and extreme transformations. In the first Act she is more akin to a wild creature than a human being; rushing about the world, a 'wild rider' as one of the squires calls her, doing errands for the knights and their ailing ruler. Then we see her early in Act Two as a weary and tormented soul, caught in an endless cycle of rebirth, enduring countless lives for a sin committed long, long ago. In another guise, also in Act Two, she is transformed into a most alluring siren, intent on leading Parsifal to moral destruction. Many other knights have already succumbed to her charms and to the powers of the magician Klingsor. Finally in Act Three, we see her as a Magdalen-like penitent. By then, she is released from her burden of sin, asks only to serve others, receives Christian baptism and helps Parsifal to fulfil his unique destiny. The soprano playing this extraordinary character must be a considerable actress as well as the most versatile of singers.

The references in Acts One and Two to Kundry's former lives remind us of the substantial Buddhist content of *Parsifal*. Wagner's sources are readily identifiable.

A collection of Buddhist legends dating from the first century AD contains the story of a Wounded Swan. The story is a recollection by the Buddha of a childhood experience in which a swan suddenly dropped from the sky and writhed on the ground in front of him in great pain. It had been hit by an arrow. The young Siddhartha (as the prince who became the Buddha was then called) pulled the arrow out and was caring for the bird when his cousin ran in excitedly, clutching his bow and arrows. The cousin ran towards the swan to claim it but Siddhartha stopped him, much to the boy's annoyance. The cousin then received a lecture on the need for compassion and its role in easing the suffering of all beings.

An almost identical event takes place in Act One of *Parsifal*. A wounded swan falls to the ground and a knight draws an arrow from its breast. Parsifal is brought before Gurnemanz clutching his bow and arrows. He joyfully admits to his skill in hitting the swan in flight. Gurnemanz then impresses on him the heartless nature of his action and does so with such poignant effect that the remorseful Parsifal breaks his bow and hurls his arrows away. In this way he learns his first lesson in compassion.

More than thirty years separated Wagner's musical depiction of the swan in *Parsifal* with that in *Lohengrin*, but there are obvious similarities. The musical themes describe not so much swans *per se* as the compassion associated with the creatures in question. The swan in *Parsifal* is obviously an object of compassion because it had been shot. However, the swan in *Lohengrin* is deserving of compassion because it is really Elsa's brother, the unfortunate Gottfried, transformed by Ortrud for her own evil intentions. The themes are as beautiful as they are moving, and I can imagine no more genuine and touching expressions of Wagner's own sense of fellow suffering.

One of the principal injunctions to a would-be follower of the Buddha is to refrain from harming all living creatures. Wagner felt passionately about the prevention of cruelty to animals. Few subjects got him more worked up. After his death in 1883, his step-daughter Daniela recorded some of his last remarks, one of which concerned a report about an elephant in Siam. It had been taking part in a festival procession and suddenly went mad and caused some damage, 'whereupon' wrote Daniela, 'the people blinded the innocent beast in the most horrible manner and tortured it to death. This brought from Papa reflections on the lamentable foolishness and wickedness of people.' His sympathies were not confined to large creatures. Cosima once noted that 'after supper he rescues a spider, "out of self interest" he says'.

Wagner vigorously opposed the use of animals for scientific experiments, and spent time (and money) during the composition of *Parsifal* supporting campaigns to prevent this. In an open letter of 1879 on vivisection, he denounced 'the scientific spectre of a soul-less age which extended from the dissecting table to the small arms factory, and made itself the patron spirit of that Utilitarian cult on which the State alone looks kindly.'[1] How prophetic he was. He was strongly opposed to hunting as a sport. As early as 1858 he had recounted in a letter to Mathilde Wesendonck his horror at witnessing a brutal scene of slaughter at a poulterer's, and made it clear to her that the theme of fellow suffering was central to his art as well as to his philosophy of life. 'This,' he told Frau Wesendonck, 'will become clearer to you some day from the third Act of *Parzival* [he still used Wolfram's spelling at that stage] which takes place on Good Friday morning.' Clearly, the central theme of compassion (*Mitleid* – literally, 'suffering with') was fixed in his mind twenty years before he began to compose the music of *Parsifal* and a quarter of a century before the work was completed.

His views were reinforced by those of Schopenhauer, who considered that the whole of morality was based on compassion, and taught that this quality was intuitive and functioned independently of the intellect.[2] It is through compassion, rather than acquired knowledge or cleverness, that the simple youth Parsifal achieves wisdom and is able to redeem others. This idea is at the very heart of *Parsifal*.

The life of the Buddha is not without relevance to the character of Parsifal. The historical Buddha lived during the sixth and fifth centuries BC. He was born Siddhartha Gautama, the son of a local chieftain in Kapilavastu on what is now the Indian-Nepalese border. What we know of him is a mixture of history, legend, mythology and mystical interpretations. Tradition has it that his father tried to divert him from his destiny by bringing him up in

---

1 An open letter to Herr Ernst von Weber, author of *The Torture-chambers of Science*, October, 1879.

2 For more on this see Brian Magee, *The Philosophy of Schopenhauer*, op.cit.

the lap of luxury, shielding him from unpleasant experiences and marrying him to his cousin, by whom he had a son. In Parsifal's case, his mother had sought to create a similarly protected life in the forest.

At some point, the Prince Siddhartha became disillusioned with the comfortable and privileged life arranged for him by his father. Leaving the palace, he was confronted for the first time by examples of sickness, old age and death. In the face of these terrible realities, the pleasures he had enjoyed seemed empty and of little value. He renounced home and family to seek the Truth, and withdrew into the forest to meditate. After meditating and undergoing terrifying ordeals he came to recognise four profound truths: that worldly reality is suffering; that the cause of suffering is desire or attachment to the things of the world; that release from suffering is possible through *Nirvana* (the 'blowing out' or extinction of the fires of greed, hatred and delusion), and that the way to this is 'the law of reality' which he called *Dharma*.

Buddhism grew out of an even older 'renouncer' tradition; that is the renunciation of the household life for the sake of the religious life and dependence upon the population at large for material needs. It is a tradition which the 'innocent fool' Parsifal also seems to be following. He had left his widowed mother and, after failing to join the glittering band of knights (symbols of worldly success) had led a solitary life. In Wagner's account, the detailed adventures recorded by Wolfram are ignored in the interests of dramatic simplicity. When Gurnemanz asks Parsifal for his name, he replies that once he had many names but he knows none of them any more. Wolfram says that Parzival had been kept entirely in ignorance of his name, but Wagner is not categorical on this point. The possibility is left open that Parsifal had deliberately blocked his name from his memory when he set out to make a new life beyond the forest. Certainly, the use of his name by Kundry triggers a vestigial memory of it.

Just as the Indian Prince Siddhartha was jolted out of ignorance by his encounters with sickness, old age and death, so the naïve youth Parsifal encounters similar images when he accompanies Gurnemanz to the Hall of the Grail. He is confronted with sickness in the person of Amfortas, in agony from the wound that never heals, symbol of the suffering that is the burden of all desire. He encounters old age in the frail personage of Titurel, who clings desperately to life through the mysteries of the Grail. In the third act, Parsifal is confronted with Titurel's corpse, ritually exposed to the knights in the depths of their despair. And so, the Buddhist imagery of suffering – sickness, old age and death – is complete.

Wolfram gives a graphic account of Parzival's journey to the Hall of the Grail and his experiences there, but Wagner is very selective in what he uses, and often adapts the details to his own purposes. The Fisher, who is described as an 'earnest, sorrowful man', tells Parzival of the castle of Munsalvaesche, and instructs him, rather prosaically, to ride on to where the rock ends, turn to the right, ascend the hill and, having arrived at the castle, bid them lower the drawbridge and let him enter. He is also warned to take care, for there are many false trails and it is easy to go astray. The first test therefore, is to find the way to Munsalvaesche – to find the way to the chosen goal. In Wagner's account, Gurnemanz tells Parsifal that no earthly path leads to Montsalvat, 'and none could tread it whom the Grail itself had not guided'. In other words, if Parsifal reaches his goal it will be in spite of himself, which is to say, in spite of his lack of sophistication, for he is the most ignorant of boys. His goal will be achieved not through worldly knowledge but intuitively, through compassion, which is the only quality really worth possessing.

In Wolfram's poem, the innocent youth arrives unaccompanied at the castle of Munsalvaesche and is courteously received and generously tended. The Queen, Rapanse de Schoye, provides

The medieval ideal of chivalry in the service of God: a knight crusader.
English drawing, c. 1250.

her own mantle of fine Arabian silk for him, and he is shown into a great hall. It is ablaze with candles and is furnished with fine carpets and a hundred couches, each with room for four knights. Anfortas is carried in on a couch and placed in front of a great fireplace. He is wrapped in furs and craves warmth, for his body is sick and, as the poet puts it, 'a painful dying was his life'.

The assembled knights suddenly break into a cry of anguish as a squire comes in carrying a lance, with blood running down the shaft and into his sleeve. The lance is carried around all four sides of the hall and is then taken out again, whereupon the wailing ceases. Maidens bring in ivory trestles and a table of precious red jacinth. Others bear two bright and sharp silver knives on napkins which they place on the table. Then the queen enters, gorgeously attired, carrying a cloth of emerald silk on which is 'the glory of Paradise, the root, stem and shoot of salvation, a thing called the Grail, a treasury of marvels beyond number'. The Grail is set before Anfortas, and then a hundred tables, each covered with a cloth of white linen, are brought in and set before the knights. Whatever food is desired, the Grail provides it, 'whatever one reached one's hand to take, it was found there before the Grail: warm food and cold, foods new and old, both cultivated and wild … For the Grail was blessing's own fruit and provided such sweet abundance that its delights were very like what we are told of the kingdom of Heaven … and for whatever drink one held one's cup, that was the drink that flowed by the power of the Grail: white wine, mulberry, or red'. Wolfram gives the Grail a Christian gloss by stating that its powers are renewed each Good Friday by a dove that descends from heaven, bearing a sacramental wafer in its beak, which it lays on the stone.

Parzival watches everything with amazement but, out of a misguided sense of reticence, refrains from asking any questions. Gornemans had advised him against being too curious (and revealing his humble origins), and so he keeps silent and waits for someone else to tell him what he needs to know. This reticence is his undoing. He is given a splendid sword, which is his cue to ask something, but he still remains silent. He does not realise that it is through his spontaneous, untutored curiosity and concern that he would restore Anfortas to health. When the meal comes to an end, the Grail is carried out by the queen and all pass out by the door through which they had entered. As they leave, Parzival catches a glimpse of the room beyond and sees there, on a couch, the most beautiful old man he has ever seen, whiter than hoar-frost.

Next morning, Parzival wakes to find his armour laid out for him, but the castle completely deserted. His horse, shield and lance await him in the courtyard but again, no-one is to be seen. Not a little put out by such treatment, he leaves the castle, and as he crosses over the drawbridge a voice calls out to him: 'Away with you, and may the sun never shine on you! A goose you are! Could you not have opened your mouth? Would that you had not been so sparing of your speech but had asked your host a question! A great prize have you forfeited!' The gates close behind him with a crash. Subsequently he learns from Sigune, his cousin, about the old Titurel and the tragic Anfortas, 'a stricken man who can neither walk nor ride nor stand nor lie, but only recline'. A simple enquiry – a gesture of concern and compassion – would lift the king's affliction. Surely, when confronted with so many marvels, he had asked about them and about the suffering which burdened the king? Sadly, Parzival admits, he had asked about none of these things. Sigune denounces him harshly – 'You beheld all the wonders of the Grail, and the silver knives and the bleeding spear ... You asked not what ailed the sore-afflicted man? You live, but you are dead to blessing.' Now all too conscious of his shortcomings, Parzival returns to the court of Arthur, where he meets the hideous sorceress Cundrie, who also denounces him. 'Ah, Munsalvaesche!' she cries, 'home of grief, woe to thee, for no man comes to thee with pity and with help'. By substituting 'sophisticated' reasons of etiquette and appearance for his intuitive concern for others, Parzival had done an unforgivable thing – he had failed to show compassion.

The epithet 'hideous' hardly does justice to Cundrie as Wolfram describes her. Her clothes are fashionable – a cape more blue than lapis lazuli, tailored in the French style, with a fine new hat from London hanging down her back – but her long black hair is as coarse as the bristles of a pig. She has a great nose, like a dog; two protruding boar's tusks, and eyebrows braided to her hair; bear's ears, a hairy face, fingernails like a lion's claws and tiny hands like a monkey's. It would indeed be a daring stage director who made Kundry in Act One of Wagner's *Parsifal* resemble her namesake in the celebrated poem by Wolfram von Eschenbach.

There is much common ground between Chrétien and Wolfram, although the former's preoccupation with chastity has been replaced by Wolfram's emphasis on charity. There are also differences in the way in which the word 'Grail' is used. The word was originally derived from the Medieval Latin *gradale*, meaning 'by degree, in stages', and was used to refer to a dish or platter that was brought to the table at various stages or servings during a meal. At the beginning of the thirteenth century, one Helinandus, a monk of Froidmont, wrote of 'a wide and somewhat hollowed-out vessel in which delicious food is served to the rich, the single pieces being arranged in rows. It is commonly called a *greal*, partly because it is pleasing to eat from, partly on account of the vessel itself which is perhaps of silver or some other precious metal, and partly because of the contents – a plentiful arrangement of delicious foods'. Chrétien spoke of a grail *(un graal)* in this sense. For Robert de Boron it became *the* Grail – the Holy Grail *(Le Saint Graal)*. Wolfram, who attached more importance to his 'macho' image as a knight than to his poetic talent, and boasted, tongue in cheek, that he knew not a single letter of the alphabet, also regarded it as *the* Grail *(der Gral)*. The old man who is briefly glimpsed in Wolfram's poem also appears in Chrétien's, where he 'is provided with a single Mass wafer, which is brought to him in the grail; and it sustains his life, such a holy thing is the grail. And he is so spiritual that he needs nothing more than the wafer contained in the grail'. In Wagner, Titurel's life is sustained by the regular uncovering of the Grail. As in Wolfram, a mere sighting of the miraculous object at regular intervals is sufficient. When Amfortas ceases to perform this rite so that he himself may die rather than live in agony, the old king dies.

In Wolfram, Parzival receives the parting insult of being called 'a goose'. Wagner makes use of this by having Gurnemanz tell Parsifal: 'In future leave the swans in peace, a gander should look for a goose!' The reference has not always been understood. Even Cosima wrote in her diary that: 'All sorts of silly things are being said about *Parsifal* ... many are shocked by the "gooseherd" – oh, dear!'[1]

Amongst the Buddhist descriptions of life after death is that of the power of unimpeded motion. A being might 'go right through rocks, hills boulders and walls' it is said, 'and in an instant can traverse any distance'. As Gurnemanz and Parsifal slowly walk, there is a gradual transformation from the forest to walls of rock, to the magnificent Hall of the Grail. They pass through woods and cliffs as if by magic, and Parsifal observes: 'I scarcely tread, yet seem already to have come far'. Gurnemanz replies with an Einsteinian (or a Buddhist) appreciation of the universe: 'You see, my son, time here becomes space'. The observation also reflects a key doctrine of Schopenhauer relating to Space, Time and Causality, which goes like this. Everything of which we are aware in our sense-experience must appear to us in

---

[1] Cosima Wagner's Diaries, ii, 3 February 1878.

spatial and temporal terms. Thus the spatio-temporal features of the world are of 'subjective' origin. They have merely relative existence because they can be exhaustively defined in terms of relations of dependence – that is, in relation to other things similarly locatable in space or time. Furthermore, both the description of the conditions under which a change is causally produced and the description of that change itself essentially involve references to spatial as well as temporal factors. Thus, causality can be said to 'unite' space and time.[1] Wagner was very familiar with Schopenhauer's writings on this subject.

When Parsifal sets out on his journey of self discovery with Gurnemanz, the staging of the mysterious transition from forest to Grail Temple can make a tremendous aural and visual impact. This was certainly the case with the first production in 1882. To achieve the unforgettable sound of the deep bells, 'swelling and dying', Wagner arranged to have built large metal canisters on wheels, rather like covered wagons from the wild west, which sat just off stage. Added to this was the sound of a new keyboard instrument, also made to the composer's specifications. Visually, the desired effect was created by using painted scenery which moved across the stage at differing speeds on rollers – fastest in the foreground, slowest at the rear – to create the (cinematic) illusion that characters were moving, even though they remained at the centre of the stage picture. Wagner probably encountered the technique in Paris, but he adapted it so successfully that the conductor Felix Weingartner, who witnessed it in 1882, felt compelled to record his amazement.

> When Gurnemanz started to lead Parsifal to the Grail Castle, I suddenly felt slightly giddy. What was happening? It seemed to me that the theatre and the whole audience were beginning to move. The scene had started to change by means of moving the backcloth. The

[1] For a full discussion of this see Patrick Gardiner, *Schopenhauer*, Penguin, 1967.

> illusion was perfect. One did not walk, one was carried. *'Zum Raum wird hier die Zeit'* ['Here time becomes space']. Corresponding scenery unrolled on two or three columns facing each other on either side of the stage, until the last cliff moved aside and the magnificently proportioned interior of the Grail Castle stood before us. Light flooded over the majestic scene precisely on the C-major chord. An incomparable effect was achieved by the simplest means.[1]

Not everything went entirely to plan in the earliest performances. For example, the music for the transition finished before all of the scenery had been unrolled. Wagner was asked to add another four minutes of music, and joked that while he had often been advised to shorten his operas, he had never before been asked to lengthen one. One of his assistants (Engelbert Humperdinck, who was later to compose *Hänsel und Gretel*) added the necessary extra bars, which were later dropped when the scenery was perfected.

What happens on stage at the end of Act One of *Parsifal* is not an enactment of the Service of Holy Communion, although many people assume that that is what they are witnessing. There is, after all, no priest to perform the office and no liturgy to follow. Amfortas is not a priest in any ecclesiastical sense, but the guardian of the Grail, who uncovers and displays it to the knights. Wagner followed medieval sources in this respect. The scene is for the benefit of Parsifal (dramatically speaking), but it is the Grail that is the centre of attention and is an 'actor' in its own right, as the medieval stories make quite clear. For Titurel, this miraculous, heavenly object is a giver of life, for Amfortas it is a source of humiliation, mortification and suffering, and for the knights it is a provider of the physical and spiritual sustenance of the holy meal. The youth who stands in a corner observing proceedings is being exposed to the Grail's mysterious workings. Gurnemanz (at least) hopes that the young simpleton will be

[1] Felix Weingartner, *Lebenserinnerungen*, Vienna, Leipzig, 1923.

sufficiently curious to seek an explanation and join in the meal. However, he just stands there like a dolt and asks nothing.

Wagner referred to the Grail scenes in *Parsifal* as 'a dream vision' and told Cosima that he was glad he had decided not to depict a Communion Service but to focus on the blessings of the Grail. He also observed that while art may use symbols to express things that cannot be expressed in any other way, this should be done in a free spirit and not in the rigid forms imposed by the church.

Parsifal was not the first (nor the last) opera in which religious symbolism was incorporated into the stage action. The Masonic rituals of *Die Zauberflöte*, for example, together with Sarastro's hymn to Isis and Osiris and the solemn processions and choruses of the priests, have much in common with the activities of the Grail Knights. In at least one case, the symbolism and dramatic impact comes very close to that of the 'meal of love' of the knights of Montsalvat. In *La Juive* (The Jewess) of 1835 by the French composer Jacques-François-Fromental Halévy, there is depicted a celebration of the feast of the Passover. It was of course on just such an occasion that Jesus met with his disciples in Jerusalem and gave them the bread and wine which were to be reminders of his presence amongst them. The expectation that Parsifal will ask the meaning of what he is witnessing in the Hall of the Grail finds a parallel in a Judaic custom at the Seder, during Passover. After the first cup has been drunk, the youngest son must ask the father about the meaning of the observance, whereupon the father replies that 'It is the sacrifice of the Lord's passover, who passed over the houses of the children of Israel in Egypt, when he smote the Egyptians, and delivered our houses. And the people bowed and worshipped.' Parsifal's failure to ask *his* question is not just an apparent failure of compassion for Amfortas but a sign of inability, or unwillingness, to identify with the others.

In the impressive second Act of Halévy's opera, we find ritual vessels and candles, a moving chant with striking rhythms, the distribution of unleavened bread, and devout supplications – all part of the stage action. Wagner knew *La Juive* well from his Paris years (1839–42) and regarded it highly. He remarked especially on its beauties, the impact of the Passover scene, the final choruses, its lively first act and the qualities of its orchestration. It contained, he said, 'the best expression of the Jewish character'. He knew Halévy personally, 'liked him very much' and arranged the piano transcription of his opera *La Reine de Chypre*. In December 1841 he wrote a newspaper article about this latter work. He praised the composer's grace and simplicity and his avoidance of 'all those pernicious fireworks and intolerable prima-donna-flourishes that had flowed from the scores of Donizetti & Co, into the pen of many a clever composer of French Opera'.[1] Halévy's music was characterised by emotive sound images, the flexible handling of solo declamation, and the blending of recitative within the melodic tissue, all of which impressed the young Wagner. On 17 January 1880, when he was working on the score of *Parsifal,* Wagner reawakened these memories by attending a performance of *La Juive* at the Teatro San Carlo in Naples.

The Grail scene in Act One is immensely impressive, but Wagner was right to liken it to a dream. It begins with the dream-like movement from the forest through the rocky wall and into the castle, and ends – again in the way of dreams – with events resolutely refusing to progress. Parsifal is unresponsive, Gurnemanz loses patience and throws the boy out, the knights are absorbed in their own reverie, and Amfortas remains trapped in his painful body. Nothing has changed. Towards the end of the scene, ethereal voices repeat the phrase *'Selig in Liebe! Selig im*

---

[1] This report appeared in the *Dresden Abend-Zeitung* of 26–29 January 1842.

Glauben!' (Blessed in love! Blessed in faith!). 'Oh, that's beautiful!' the composer had cried out to Cosima during its composition in January 1878. 'Exactly as I wanted it.' And so, amidst this music of great beauty, the scene closes quietly, with a message of hope for those willing to listen.

In Europe in the nineteenth century, the custom of artists taking curtain calls after each act was a common one, and it still occurs in certain houses in Europe and America. However, Wagner decided (in consultation with his singers) to dispense with this custom for *Parsifal,* since he was anxious that nothing should break the dramatic spell until the very end. Like Klingsor, he too was in the business of illusion. This innovation had not come out of the blue, although that is the impression one sometimes gets from modern commentaries. The reality is that Wagner had spent much of his life trying to change the audience's relationship to the drama, and the design of the *Festspielhaus* reflects his efforts in this regard as much as his concern with acoustics and aesthetics. It is to him, for example, that we owe the now universal practice of turning off the auditorium lights and maintaining silence during a performance.

In the late eighteenth and early nineteenth centuries, going to the opera was primarily a social event and, as a young man, Wagner had observed with disgust the way in which opera music had become merely an article of fashion. The whole opera-going experience had become a farce and artists were treated abominably. The worst instances were to be found in Italy, where audience members came and went as they pleased, talked freely, and (if they occupied a box) ate and drank, gambled, made love and generally regarded what happened on the stage as a spectator sport. Encores were expected regardless of the artistic violence done to the drama, and audiences would brook no refusals. On one occasion the soprano Caterina Gabrielli, near the end of a glorious career, fell foul of her audience for not meeting its demands for an encore, and was driven from the stage by a cacophony of coughing and nose blowing followed by a torrent of abuse.[1]

Berlioz attended a performance of Donizetti's *L'elisir d'amore* at La Scala in Milan, which he described in the following terms:

> People were talking in normal voices with their backs to the stage. The singers, undeterred, gesticulated and yelled their lungs out in the strictest spirit of rivalry. At least I presumed they did from their wide open mouths, but the noise of the audience was such that no sound penetrated except from the bass drum. People were gambling, eating supper in their boxes etc. etc. Consequently, perceiving it was useless to hear anything of the score, which was then new to me, I left.

German houses were not quite as bad, but the expectations of their audiences were much the same. Wagner was determined that opera should be restored to a serious place in the artistic firmament. He developed a continuous melodic style – neither aria nor recitative – which demanded the audience's whole attention and, incidentally, left no room for encores. In Italy, encores continued to be a common occurrence until well into the twentieth century, when Toscanini (a great Wagner conductor) refused to allow them on artistic grounds.

The first production of *Der Ring des Nibelungen* in August 1876 was an epoch-making event in many ways, including in terms of audience standards. However, the old habits were to die hard, and those who attended the first cycles at Bayreuth behaved, more or less, as opera audiences were used to behaving. They talked, they laughed and they applauded during the performance! Nevertheless, they sensed that new constraints and expectations were being applied – the theatre was in darkness,

[1] See also John Rosselli, 'Opera as a Social Occasion' in *The Oxford History of Opera*, edited by Roger Parker, Oxford University Press, 1994.

they were forced to look at the stage (rather than each other), and the seating arrangements prevented them from moving around before the end of the act. Wagner also decided that there should be no curtain calls until the end of the opera, a decision that irritated some of the singers who expected the normal practice to be followed.

So burdensome were the financial losses incurred on the 1876 *Ring* production and the completion of the *Festspielhaus*, that further Bayreuth performances were out of the question until 1882. For six years the revolutionary theatre stood silent and empty. Wagner's earliest opportunity to reintroduce audience practices that he felt were appropriate to serious art came with *Parsifal*. This time he made sure that his singers were 'on side' on the matter of curtain calls. However, it was not quite so easy to get his audiences to understand why they too had to change their ways. When he explained that there would be no curtain calls, they became confused. Should they applaud or shouldn't they? Most decided to remain in total silence throughout, and those exuberant souls who did clap were roundly hissed for their pains. The issue became an embarrassment and a distraction. This was not what Wagner had intended. Cosima in her diary entry for 26 July 1882 wrote:

> When, after the second act, there is much noise and calling, R. comes to the balustrade, says that though the applause is very welcome to his artists and to himself, they had agreed, in order not to impinge on the impression, not to take a bow, so that there would be no curtain calls ... But at the end R. is vexed by the silent audience, which has misunderstood him; he once again addresses it from the gallery, and when the applause then breaks out and there are continual calls, R. appears in front of the curtain and says that he tried to assemble the artists, but they were by now half undressed.

When the composer himself shouted 'Bravo!' to the Flower Maidens, whose singing was judged to be 'beyond praise', he was not recognised in the darkness and he too was hissed! Nevertheless, he continued to shout 'Bravo!' over the heads of the audience at every performance he attended during the season.

To this day, those Bayreuth patrons who have the temerity to applaud at the end of the first act are met with a barrage of hisses, as if they had been caught spitting in church. Some never recover from the humiliation and do not return for Act Two, which is a tragedy. In an attempt to deal with this problem without upsetting the die-hards, the following notice was printed in the Bayreuth program book for 1967:

> As many complaints have been made that a part of the audience attempts by hissing to prevent the applause after the acts of *Parsifal,* the Committee think it advisable to publish the wishes of the Master himself in this respect. The quiet finish of the first act precludes, of course [*sic*], any applause; but the Master himself wished that after the second and third acts the audience might show their thanks to the artists by applause. The re-opening of the curtain has been arranged by the Master's desire, and it will, therefore, be continued.

Actually, as far as the withholding of applause after the first act is concerned, Cosima's diary suggests that this 'evolved' but was not what Wagner had originally intended. It seems that he merely wanted to dampen the usual expectations of curtain calls before the end, when it would be appropriate for the singers to step out of character. On 28 July 1882 Cosima wrote: 'After the first act there is a reverent silence, which has a pleasant effect. But when, after the second, the applauders are again hissed, it becomes embarrassing.' The matter was still a concern (but seemed to have resolved itself) on 30 July when she wrote: 'Again silence after the first act, great applause after the 2nd act; calls after the 3rd act and the curtain rises on the final tableau.' And so the tradition was established.

It is widely believed that the reason for the self-imposed silence after Act One is the 'sacred' nature of the scene – which of course is nonsense, particularly in view of the derivation of the 'thing called the Grail', to use Wolfram's words. The experience of people hissing or being hissed at after the curtain falls adds nothing to a great work of art, and certainly detracts from it. To those who encourage this practice, the closing words of Gurnemanz seem particularly apt: 'Off with you, be on your way! In future leave the swans in peace, a gander should look for a goose!'

Words cannot give you

anywhere near the

tremendous impression,

shattering yet life-enhancing,

which this work

made on me.

ALBAN BERG

Illusion and Desire

Act Two opens with the agitated, dazzling music of the magician Klingsor who is in his tower, sitting before a metal mirror, surrounded by instruments of necromancy. In the mirror he sees Parsifal approaching and summons a reluctant Kundry to work her wiles on the innocent boy. The idea that Klingsor should use a mirror to witness Parsifal's fall from grace is an interesting one, not to be found in Wolfram's Parzival. The equivalent imagery in that work relates to a magic pillar, which is discovered by the knight Gawan in *Schastel marveile*, the castle of wonders belonging to the magician Clinschor. By means of this pillar, it is possible to see what is happening in the lands all around. A mirror, on the other hand, features in Buddhist scriptures. In these we read of the King of the Dead, who holds up to each being a shining mirror wherein all their deeds are reflected. The scriptures add that 'the mirror in which he seems to read your past is your own memory, and also his judgment is your own. It is you yourself who pronounce your own judgment, which in turn determines your next rebirth'. So it is that Parsifal, through a test of his moral courage, will now determine his own fate.

Wolfram's magic pillar enables Gawan to discover that, amongst four hundred queens and four hundred maidens whom Clinschor keeps captive in *Schastel marveile*, are his grandmother, mother and two sisters. Such prosaic scraps of information were of no use to Wagner and he ignored them. However, again the Buddhist sources proved more fruitful. Amongst the legends of the Buddha is the story of Mara, the tempter figure whose baits are the pleasures of the senses. Mara had tried to defeat the Buddha before he had achieved enlightenment, saying to his followers:

> Look over there at that sage, clad in the armour of determination, with truth and spiritual virtue as his weapons, the arrows of his intellect drawn ready to shoot. If he should succeed in overcoming me and proclaiming the way to final benediction, then my realm would be empty. So far he has not won the eye of full knowledge and is within my sphere of influence. While there is time I will attempt to break his solemn purpose.

But, continues the legend, Mara, his army and his seductive daughters were defeated and fled in all directions – 'their rocks, logs and trees scattered everywhere'.

In the course of Parsifal's quest, he encounters Klingsor with his knights and beguiling Flower Maidens. Klingsor says to Kundry: 'Now today we have the most dangerous to meet; the shield of foolishness protects him.' Watching Parsifal in his mirror, he comments: 'Whatever the prophecies say, too young and foolish, you fall into my power. Once stripped of your purity you will become my slave!' The connection between Wagner's text and the Mara legend are clear.

Parsifal overcomes the knights, resists the maidens, and recovers the Holy Spear when Klingsor hurls it at him. Miraculously, the spear remains poised above Parsifal's head. In Buddhist legend, it was not a spear but a discus (some say thunderbolt) that was thrown by Mara at the meditating Buddha. This missile was transformed into a canopy of flowers that remained suspended over the Buddha's head. Klingsor, like Mara, is defeated and, according to the stage directions, the castle sinks 'as if by an earthquake' and the garden withers to a desert; or as the Mara legend puts it 'rocks, logs and trees are scattered everywhere'.

At the beginning of the act, Kundry is summoned by her master Klingsor and reminded of her previous lives as the Nordic messenger Gundryggia and the biblical Herodias. She is a tormented creature, longing for sleep and death but condemned to endless reincarnations. In a former life she had laughed at the Saviour as he hung dying on the cross. Her sin was of the gravest kind because it was the very antithesis of compassion, directed towards Christ himself in his moment of suffering. His own compassionate gaze fell on her, she says, and now she seeks him again 'from world to world'.

The Buddha taught that human beings are responsible for their own destiny, and determine it by their own deeds from one life to the next. He taught that they wander through the vast endless universe, attempting to find some permanent home, a place where they can feel secure. In the realms of the gods they find great joy, and in the worlds of hell great suffering, but their sojourn in these places is always temporary. Their search for happiness and security within the round of rebirth never ends. Kundry is in just such a predicament. Even Parsifal acknowledges a state of reincarnation, declaring in the final Act: 'Ah! What transgression, what burden of guilt must my foolish head have borne from eternity, since no repentance, no atonement can free me from my blindness.'

We have learnt from Gurnemanz in Act One the story of Klingsor's self-mutilation, carried out in his futile attempt to be admitted to the company of the Grail Knights. Clinschor, his equivalent in Wolfram's poem, has also been castrated, but not by his own hand. In the thirteenth-century version, we are told (by Gawan's grandmother) that the magician was once a great noble of Capua. He offered himself in service (this is a euphemism) to the Queen of Sicily. When the king discovered them together 'one cut of a knife made him a capon'. Clinschor then fled to a city called Persidia, where magic was first invented, and returned equipped with his magic arts. Because of the shame he had suffered, he was filled with hatred for everyone. It became his greatest pleasure to rob those who are happiest of their joy, especially those who are honoured and respected. In Wagner's *Parsifal*, Kundry, despite her enslavement to Klingsor, knows exactly how to put salt on the magician's wounds, so to speak. When he says that he is the only one with whom her wiles do not work, she replies with a shrill laugh 'Ha ha! Are you chaste?' Ouch!

The Buddhist texts contain graphic descriptions of Paradise, a place where beings go as a reward for especially worthy past lives, before returning to the world and the inevitable cycle of suffering. One account describes the giant flowers that grow in that celestial place 'some half a mile in circumference, others up to ten miles.' Another account tells how 'celestial nymphs with their playfulness captivate the wearied minds of those ascetics who had, in their life on earth, decided to purchase Paradise by first paying the price in austerities'. We read of the nymphs' 'soft words, tremulous calls, wanton swayings, sweet laughter, butterfly kisses and seductive glances.' The descriptions could easily apply to Klingsor's Magic Garden and its inhabitants.

In the stage directions for Act Two, Wagner describes the sudden appearance of the garden and the Flower Maidens who, with Kundry, offer the 'innocent fool' a glimpse of Paradise. When Parsifal approaches Klingsor's tower, it sinks rapidly and the garden rises and fills the whole stage. There is a long pause when Parsifal enters the garden. 'Ah! Music!' said Wagner. ''What could take its place? In spoken dialogue this pause would be impossible. The *speaking pause* is the property of music.' The garden, we are told in the stage directions, comprises tropical vegetation (wondrously strange, even in northern Spain where the action is set) and a luxuriant display of flowers. The directions also require the maidens to assume the appearance of flowers and, in the original production, their costumes represented giant flowers.[1] At one point, Wagner wanted to call them 'Flowers' rather than 'Flower Maidens' because he thought the latter made them sound like flower sellers! The scenery was also a collection of enormous and brightly coloured flowers – albeit somewhat less than half a mile in circumference! Wagner made it clear that the scene should not be a repeat of the Venusberg. These Maidens (but not Kundry) are as children; their laughter is the unthinking laughter of children and their attractions are simply as nature provided. 'My girls shall rush in with a wail, like children whose toys have been taken away – without anger,' he said. 'Innocence should be the keynote of everything.' Just as flowers are intended to attract insects to themselves, so the Flower Maidens cannot help attracting hapless wayfarers like Parsifal into their embraces. Parsifal even says to them 'How sweet you smell. Are you flowers then?' On one occasion, Wagner told Cosima that he would treat them like saplings – this had been suggested to him by the melody of his chorus. He said he wanted to present them as languishing figures, not as demons.

In composing the music for the Flower Maidens, Wagner began by working out the contrapuntal vocal writing on four or five staves and then wrote the words for it, just as he had done with the finale of the first act of *Lohengrin* and the complicated street fight in the second act of *Die Meistersinger*. Of the gently swaying, hypnotic chorus *'Komm, komm, holder Knabe!'* (Come, come, handsome boy!) he remarked 'In the first act I was very sparing with the more sensuous intervals but now I'm using my old paint pot again.' Cosima noted in her diary that, on 23 August 1878, Wagner played this music for Liszt, and that 'This captivates my father at once, R. fetches the manuscript, and then the whole second act up to the kiss is gone through, R. thrilled by the

[1] Felix Weingartner described the 1882 costumes as 'incomprehensibly tasteless' but the singing as 'beyond praise'.

fascination the divine work exerts on my father and radiating genius, greatness, kindness!'

The Buddhist scriptures tell us that Paradise is only temporary, that it gives no real freedom, holds no security, cannot be trusted and gives no lasting satisfaction. In other words, its charms are as transitory as Klingsor's garden that vanishes into the desert. In 1868, when Wagner was reconsidering the possibility of a music drama on the subject of *Die Sieger*, he made extensive notes in his diary, the so-called 'Brown Book', about the Buddhist notion of a transitory Paradise and the inevitable return to the world of drudgery and suffering. It was clearly a subject that was on his mind when *Parsifal* was taking shape. The first detailed prose draft of the entire work had been completed in 1865 and is also to be found in the 'Brown Book'.

The scene between Parsifal and Kundry in Act Two is the acme of operatic seductions. The beguiling, caressing line of Kundry's voice and the fragrant, intoxicating orchestration predates by decades Richard Strauss's soprano writing in *Salome* and *Der Rosenkavalier* and the last songs. Even sixty years later, Strauss was able to remark: 'As for *Parsifal* and the *Ring*, I must have heard them some fifty times (usually when rehearsing and conducting them myself) ... and yet every time I discover new beauties and new revelations.' Debussy, too, was quick to acknowledge the inspiration that he drew from Wagner's last opera, and wrote of 'orchestral certainties such as I have encountered only in *Parsifal*'.

Parsifal's attention is drawn to Kundry in Act Two when, amidst the delightful confusion of his encounter with the Flower Maidens, she calls his name. This is the first time that we have heard his name out loud, and the effect is electrifying. We see her at her most bewitching, in a totally new form. She is, as the stage directions put it, 'a youthful woman of great beauty, lying on a bed of flowers wearing revealing, fanciful garments'. How revealing is

Wagner imagined Klingsor's Kundry as 'lying there naked, like a Titian Venus.' *The Venus of Urbino* by Titian (1477–1576). Uffizi Gallery, Florence.

revealing? When the designer of the original production, Paul von Joukowsky, produced a sketch of the Act Two Kundry in 1881, Wagner expressed satisfaction with it but added, 'Actually, she should be lying there naked, like a Titian Venus!'

In the Cistercian *Queste del Saint Graal*, Perceval is roused from sleep one moonlight night by a seductress standing over him, inviting him to join her on adventure. He makes the sign of the Cross, and with a cry she vanishes in a burst of flame. The practice of banishing dark forces by making the sign of the Cross is used for dispatching Klingsor at the end of Act Two. The seductress in Perceval's encounter is perpetuated by Kundry, who is obviously an expert in the seductive arts. It was she who, in her glamorous form, had seduced Amfortas at the time of his wounding, although he failed to make the connection in Act One, when he thanked the dishevelled creature for her charity and loyalty. Now she will work her charms on Parsifal. Her first tactic is to weaken his defences. She awakens memories of his past, explaining that she had known him even before his birth,[1] and had given him the Arabic name[2] chosen by his dying father. Then she strikes at his self-esteem by revealing how his mother, Herzeleide, had died, waiting for his return – 'sorrow broke her heart, and Heart's Sorrow died.' Predictably, Parsifal, is mortified by his own insensitivity. Stricken with guilt, he accuses himself of his sweet mother's murder. If only he could make amends! Kundry offers a way; for she brings (from his mother of course) a farewell kiss. At this point we might recall Herzeloyde's own advice to Parzival in Wolfram's poem – 'strive to win a good lady's ring, and then kiss and embrace her'. No wonder Kundry has invoked memories of his mother. Parsifal is intensely vulnerable, and his sexual feelings are being subtly aroused. Their lips meet in a long kiss. Then he reacts with a gesture of utmost terror, clutching his heart as if trying to master an agonising pain. In a loud voice he cries out 'Amfortas! The wound! The wound!'

What *is* going on here? Siegfried awakened Brünnhilde with a kiss – his first kiss, and his first (ever) encounter with a woman. He had never even *seen* a woman before, so he had more reason than most to be surprised. However, Siegfried's eventual reaction had been one of delirious joy. Why should Parsifal behave so oddly? We can approach the scene on two levels; firstly, a literal one. Parsifal is suddenly conscious of Kundry's strategy of entrapment, the tragedy that befell Amfortas, and the origin and nature of the wound. He describes in almost voyeuristic detail his inner vision of the seduction of the Grail King, and is obviously experi-

[1] Just as Brünnhilde tells Siegfried that she had cared for him before he was born.

[2] Kundry's explanation of his name is fictitious, as Wagner admitted to Cosima. He added that probably there would not be many orientalists in the audience.

encing passion because 'everything trembles, quakes and quivers in sinful desire'. However, it dawns on him that his soul is in mortal danger.

When the serpent tempted Eve (and through her, Adam) to eat the fruit of the tree in the midst of the Garden of Eden, he said: 'Ye shall not surely die: for God doth know that in the day ye eat thereof, then your eyes shall be opened, and ye shall be as gods, knowing good and evil.' Kundry (under Klingsor's spell) tells Parsifal: 'The full embrace of my love then would raise you to godhead. Redeem the world, if this is your destiny; make yourself a god for an hour ...' However, on this occasion the 'serpent's' plans go badly awry, for Parsifal resists, and calls on the Saviour to help him. It is Klingsor who is banished, and Kundry who is freed from the bondage of her ancient sin. Kundry's sensuous form is an illusion; as much a product of Klingsor's magic as is the shimmering garden that vanishes with him. It is not in fact Kundry whom Parsifal rejects but an evil phantasm. It is not Kundry herself who confronts Parsifal but Klingsor. It is not the kiss of a mother's love that he receives but Klingsor's kiss of death.

An interesting parallel can be drawn with the assumption of Gunther's form by Siegfried in *Götterdämmerung*, in order to win Brünnhilde for Gunther. Although Klingsor has not actually assumed Kundry's physical form, he has certainly created a new persona for her and his spirit has possessed her. However, there are very different outcomes. Siegfried/Gunther succeeds in mastering Brünnhilde by brute force, and only later does she comprehend the deception and its consequences. Klingsor/Kundry fails to master Parsifal by seduction because he comprehends the deception and its consequences at the moment of the kiss.

Parsifal 'enters a complete trance' and begins to call on the Saviour. He remembers the scene in the hall of the Grail, which is now beginning to make sense. Kundry, still the temptress, takes up his theme. She recalls her own memory of the Saviour, who had turned his gaze on her in pity when, in a former life, she had mocked him on the cross. She longs for redemption, she says; Parsifal is just the one to provide it, and one hour is all that it will take! Parsifal replies that after one hour together they would both be damned for evermore. Her redemption, for which he has been sent, comes from a very different source. Then Parsifal asks to be shown the way to Amfortas, and Kundry erupts with fury and with a venom that suggests that it is really Klingsor's voice that we are hearing: 'Let the fallen one perish … he fell by his own spear!'[1] Parsifal has had a lucky escape.

Now for a more philosophical explanation. The moral defeat of Amfortas and the moral victory of Parsifal are two aspects of a single parable. The lesson of this parable is that suffering is inevitable when desire, rather than compassion, governs human actions. Desire may take many forms, although sexual desire in particular is a powerful and universal manifestation. Desire can overwhelm other sensibilities. It can make us do things which, in our heart of hearts, we do not intend to do. It can maim and disfigure us emotionally. The parable of Kundry, Amfortas and Parsifal is, therefore, an illustration of those fundamental truths first recognised by the Buddha: that worldly existence is suffering, and that the cause of this suffering is desire and attachment to worldly things. However, the Buddha also taught that release from suffering is possible through the 'blowing out' of the fires of greed, hatred and delusion. Klingsor had revealed the means by which Kundry could achieve this release when he told her 'He that rejects you will set you free.' By rejecting every stratagem and enticement that Kundry can devise, Parsifal not only frees himself from the wounding affliction of desire but also 'blows out' the fires of Kundry's suffering. He is therefore, truly the instrument of her redemption.

---

1 The 'real' Kundry's attitude towards Amfortas had been very different in Act One.

However, the story does not end there. If salvation depended on ourselves alone, none would be saved, for human beings are fallible. However, Jesus Christ by his supreme act of compassion for the world, offered himself as a sufficient sacrifice on the cross. Through him, the relationship between God and man, lost when Adam and Eve were banished from the Garden of Eden, has been restored. St Paul ('the first Christian' as Wagner called him) was the first to write about this parallel in his Letter to the Romans, making the observation that: 'For as by one man's disobedience many were made sinners, so by the obedience of one shall many be made righteous.' The medieval legend of Adam reinforces the connection by insisting that Adam was buried on Golgotha, where Jesus was later crucified.[1] Kundry's long search for Christ is over, for she has been released from her suffering by the triumph of compassion over desire. It only remains for her to be reconciled to Christ through baptism. This is the point that we have reached when the curtain rises on Act Three.

[1] For this reason, some manuscripts even depict the Grail as a coffin.

His last work was a prayer.

In his heart he

dedicated Parsifal

to the everlasting God.

Wagner could not

pray liturgically,

and so in this way

he created his own prayer.

Franz Liszt

The Day of Innocence

The author of a work known as *The Lancelot Grail*, claimed that on the eve of Good Friday in the year 717, he received a book on the Grail and other matters from Christ himself. Good Friday seems to have been an especially propitious day in medieval times for the occurrence of such events, and features frequently in literature. Even in Dante's *Divine Comedy*, the poet set out on his spiritual journey on the vigil of Good Friday. In Wolfram's *Parzival*, we read that each Good Friday, a dove brought a consecrated wafer from Heaven to lay upon the Grail and renew its powers. This is, no doubt, the origin of the final stage direction in Wagner's *Parsifal*, according to which (on Good Friday) a white dove descends and hovers over Parsifal's head.

In Chrétien's *Perceval*, there is an account of several knights being shocked by the fact that Perceval appears in his armour on Good Friday, for on that day it is not appropriate to carry arms. The knights have just returned from visiting a hermit, who has heard their confessions and given them absolution. Perceval weeps and asks directions to the hermit. When the meeting takes place, he tells the hermit that he has been wandering for five years and has quite forgotten God. It was his failure to ask a question about the bleeding lance and the Grail that had weighed heavily on him and caused him to abandon his faith. Wagner drew on many of these details. We find Gurnemanz living a hermit-like existence on the edge of the forest when he is visited by a down-cast and weary Parsifal, wearing black armour. Parsifal is chastised for being armed on Good Friday, Gurnemanz telling

The shining tranquility of the Good Friday landscape
was anticipated in *The Baptism of Christ* by Piero della Francesca
(1410/20–1492), National Gallery, London.

him 'Do not offend the Lord, who today, bereft of all arms, offered his holy blood to redeem the sinful world!' Parsifal reveals his identity and recounts the story of his wanderings, including his recovery of the Holy Spear that he has kept undefiled.

Wagner claimed in his autobiography *Mein Leben*, that in 1857 in Zürich, he had been inspired by a beautiful Good Friday to write down his earliest ideas for *Parsifal*. He subsequently qualified this by saying that the day had not actually been Good Friday, but that he had thought to himself at the time, 'This is how Good Friday ought to be.' Poetic enthusiasm had become poetic licence (which, he added, was also the case with some of his supposed love affairs!). Nevertheless, it was the idea of Good Friday that had captured his imagination and had provided a link to the old legends.

Gurnemanz waxes lyrical about the animals, and even the flowers and grasses of the meadow which 'give thanks' for that particular day. Some writers have found much merriment in the latter sentiment, but the key to the passage lies in the last few lines: 'Thus all creation gives thanks, all that here blooms and soon fades, now that nature, absolved from sin, today gains its day of innocence.' The underlying idea is that because of the sacrifice of Christ (the second Adam as he is sometimes described), all of God's creation had been restored to a state of innocence.

In 1849, a warrant was issued in Dresden for the arrest of Richard Wagner for revolutionary activities. With Liszt's help, he fled into exile in Switzerland. During the first months of that tumultuous year, Wagner had sketched the scenario for a five-act opera called *Jesus von Nazareth*. This work never advanced past the scenario stage, but it depicted Jesus as a social revolutionary. Wagner tells us in his autobiography that 'Inspired by a recent reading of the gospels, I had at that time just produced a sketch for a tragedy to be performed in the ideal theatre of the future and to be entitled *Jesus von Nazareth*'. Clearly then, his biblical sources (as distinct from his socialist ones) were the gospels themselves. The singer Dietrich Fischer-Dieskau records in his autobiography[1] that he once had occasion to examine Wagner's Dresden library, assembled during the composer's revolutionary days and forfeited when he had fled into exile at the age of thirty-six. Fischer-Dieskau discovered to his surprise that the book which carried the greatest number of marginal notations was the Bible.

Jesus von Nazareth had not been Wagner's first attempt to set biblical material to music. In 1843 he had written *Das Liebesmahl der Apostel* ('The Meal of Love of the Apostles'), a 'biblical scene' for adult male chorus and large orchestra, composed to his own text for a choral festival at Dresden. Its subject was Pentecost, when the Holy Spirit had descended on the Apostles; a subject that would be used again sixty years later by Gustav Mahler in the great choral opening to his Eighth Symphony. It contains some impressive writing that foreshadows, in a limited way, both *Lohengrin* and *Parsifal.* Wagner never suffered from self-delusion as far as his compositions were concerned. In his autobiography he wrote:

> I was not displeased with it when it was done, more especially when it was played at the rehearsals given by the Dresden Choral Society under my personal supervision. When, therefore, 1200 singers from all parts of Saxony gathered around me in the *Frauenkirche,* I was astonished at the comparatively feeble effect produced on my ear by this colossal human tangle of sounds. The conclusion at which I arrived was that these enormous choral undertakings are folly, and I never again felt inclined to repeat the experiment.

By contrast, the Prelude to Act Three of *Parsifal* took Western music into regions that were even stranger and more remote than those of *Tristan*. Cosima said of it: 'It begins like the lament of

[1] Dietrich Fischer-Dieskau, *Echoes of a Lifetime*. Macmillan, 1989.

an extinguished star, after which one discerns, like gestures, Parsifal's arduous wanderings and Kundry's pleas for salvation.' Wagner explained that his preludes 'must all be elemental, not dramatic like the *Leonore* Overtures, for that makes the drama superfluous'. He composed slowly and deliberately, sometimes just ten bars in a day; a whole morning could be spent on a modulation. Smooth transition was the guiding rule; nothing was to be jarring. Sometimes a single note was a cause for celebration, as on the occasion when he described the entry of the kettledrum in G at the point of Kundry's baptism as 'the finest thing I have ever done'. To him it was the 'obliteration of the whole being, of all earthly desire.' He took great pleasure in what he called the 'elegy' – that process within Parsifal's soul when he becomes once again 'an ordinary mortal' before he becomes a king. 'You have no idea of all the things in it', he told Cosima. The spirit of Bach was never far from Wagner when he was composing Act Three. There were regular Bach evenings at *Wahnfried*, and the *48 Preludes and Fugues* were frequently invoked and analysed. 'That is music in its true essence,' he said. 'Everything we compose is applied music.'

The spiritual light that illuminates *Das Liebesmahl der Apostel* and even the embryonic *Jesus von Nazareth*, has its source in the gospels. But in the case of *Parsifal*, that light is refracted through the prism of the medieval mind. At first glance, Act Three contains features that seem merely replications of biblical events: Kundry washes Parsifal's feet and dries them with her hair, Parsifal is anointed with costly oil, Gurnemanz blesses Parsifal, and Parsifal baptises Kundry. However, we can also recognise in such details something of the theological parallelism that so fascinated medieval artists and poets, when they drew comparisons between the Old Testament and the New, and between biblical happenings and later events. In one episode of Robert de Boron's *Joseph d'Arimathie* for example, Christ tells Joseph:

> The Enemy, who does nothing save to lie in wait for people to incite them to evil, first seduced Eve because he saw that woman was weaker in spirit than man; and because all mankind was reduced to captivity by a woman, God desired that all should be freed once more by a woman (namely the Virgin Mary). As the trunk bore the apple that grew from the tree by the miracle of God, so too had the Son of God to die upon the wood, in order to accomplish this salvation.

Thus we may, in the same spirit, draw comparisons between Kundry in the Magic Garden and Eve in the Garden of Eden (and between Klingsor and the Serpent), Kundry and the Magdalen, Parsifal and Adam, and so on. However, Wagner was adamant about one comparison that had been suggested to him – Parsifal should not be compared with Christ. 'There was no thought of the Saviour in my mind,' he told Cosima, and on another occasion: 'Jesus as a tenor; what an appalling thought!'

In Wolfram's poem, Parzival baptises not Cundrie but his elder half-brother, the pied black and white Feirefiz, who is a Muslim. Initially, Feirefiz cannot even see the Grail, only the beautiful Queen Repanse de Schoye, sister of Anfortas, who is carrying it. The old Titurel sends a message to say that 'If he is a heathen unbaptised, there is no use for him to associate with those who do see the Grail. For him there is a veil around it.' Feirefiz decides that if baptism will help his chances in love, he will embrace the new religion. The Grail itself fills the baptismal font with water that is 'neither too warm nor too cold', and when Feirefiz is baptised, the Grail at last becomes visible to him. On the stone now appear the words:

> ANY TEMPLAR APPOINTED BY GOD'S HAND TO BE MASTER OVER A FOREIGN FOLK MUST FORBID THE ASKING OF HIS NAME OR RACE AND HELP THEM TO THEIR RIGHTS. BUT IF THE QUESTION IS ASKED OF HIM, THEY SHALL NO LONGER HAVE HIS HELP.

Eventually, Feirefiz departs for India to become a 'master over a foreign folk', where his new bride, Repanse de Schoye, gives birth to a son who will become Prester John. The Grail's injunction will also, in time, apply to Parsifal's son, Lohengrin.

Wagner's conductor for the first production of *Parsifal* was Hermann Levi, a Jew and the son of the chief rabbi in Giessen. At one point during rehearsals, Wagner went through one of his more tactless and perverse phases, trying to persuade Levi to be baptised and then 'we shall both take communion together!' Did he think that, like Feirefiz, Levi too was unable to see the Grail? The good-natured Levi tolerated this latest idiocy, and his affection and respect for Wagner remained to the end. He wrote to his father 'Wagner is the best and noblest of men ... I thank God daily for the privilege to be close to such a man. It is the most beautiful experience of my life.' He was with the Wagners in Venice until the day before the composer died. In a subsequent letter to his father he reported: 'On Monday midday I left Venice, the Master accompanied me to the stairs, kissed me several times – I was much moved – and 24 hours later!'

The Knights of the Grail, the inhabitants of Montsalvat, have been the object of much conjecture and interpretation in recent times. Some contemporary writers claim to detect in this knightly band such lurid qualities as a celebration of Aryan racial purity, anti-Semitism and homo-eroticism. Scandal there may be in the off-stage lives of the Grail Knights, but to overlay this with a gloss of twentieth-century politics or even late nineteenth-century speculation about race (including Wagner's after 1881), is to distort *Parsifal* beyond reason.

The historical Christian role-models for the Grail Knights were the Poor Knights of Christ and of the Temple of Solomon (the Knights Templar). Wolfram refers to the Grail Knights as *Templeise,* and his mentor Kyot was said to have stayed in Jerusalem and to have had personal experience of the Templars. The

Order was founded about 1118 or, in other words, about sixty years before Chrétien de Troyes' *Perceval* and eighty years before Wolfram von Eschenbach's *Parzival*. They were formally recognised by the Church at the Council of Troyes in 1128, and that great enthusiast for the Crusades, St Bernard of Clairvaux, was commissioned to write the Rule by which they should live. Their original purpose was to safeguard pilgrims going to Jerusalem, and they were headquartered in a palace near the site of Solomon's temple. In the Holy Land they became a source of much trouble to the Christian King of Jerusalem, for they answered directly to the Pope, and they constantly violated treaties with the Muslim powers. After a battle of 1187 (that is, shortly before Wolfram began work on *Parzival*), Saladin made an example of captured Templars by beheading them all while sparing his other prisoners. Wagner described Klingsor's castle as being 'in a rich Arabian style'.

Although the Templars began as an order of poverty and humility (symbolised on their seal by two of them riding on the same horse) they acquired great wealth and influence in Europe. Their property was not subject to taxes and tithes and they were not subject to secular law, since they answered only to the Pope. Such privileges attracted envy and resentment, and King Philip 'the Fair' of France and his chancellor devised a plan to get their hands on the Order's wealth. In 1307, the Grand Master was summoned to Europe where allegations of blasphemy, sorcery and other crimes, including sexual improprieties, were made. Nearly all of the Templars in France were arrested and, under torture or threat of torture, confessed to a variety of crimes ranging from spitting or urinating on the crucifix to sodomy. Many of these confessions were subsequently retracted but the damage was already done. Pope Clement V reluctantly issued a papal bull in 1312 suppressing the Order. Philip burnt the Grand Master and other Templars at the stake, and other acts of cruelty were committed. Although the Order's property in Germany went to their companion Order, the Hospitallers, most of that in France and England went to the Crown.

When a would-be Templar sought admission to the Order, he had to show that he believed in the holy Catholic faith, had been born legitimate and of a knightly family, was not married or in holy orders, was not in debt, was of sound body and had not bribed anyone to gain admission. He swore to obey the Master of the Temple and other superior officers, to preserve chastity and the good usages and the good customs of the Order, to own no property, to protect, defend and enlarge the kingdom of Jerusalem and never to permit Christians to be murdered or unjustly disinherited, and not to leave the Order without permission.[1] The daily activities of the knights were governed by the canons of the Cistercian Rule and included a full round of religious services beginning with matins and ending after supper with compline at nine o'clock, and the drinking of a cup of wine and water. What we see of the ceremonies in Montsalvat, while alien to modern experience, is in keeping with a medieval religious military Order, of which the Knights Templar were the pre-eminent example. The Grail Castle of legend may be thought of as a kind of heavenly Jerusalem, as various writers have observed.

Although the motivation for crushing the Templars contained a good measure of greed and resentment on the part of European rulers, and especially the French King, there is also some evidence that the Templars were, after nearly two centuries in the East, susceptible to Islam and to Gnosticism – a compound of Christianity, Hellenic philosophy, eastern mysticism and magic. There is no smoke without fire, as they say, and involvement with such heresies would certainly have provided a pretext to

---

[1] Note the comment by Amfortas in Act One of *Parsifal* about Gawan's departure without permission.

move against them. The vulnerability of the Templars, like that of the Grail Knights, to 'heathen influences' in a variety of forms was a real one and could end in disaster, as they discovered in 1307.

Wagner's inspiration can, therefore, be traced through Wolfram and Chrétien to the religious military Orders of the Crusades, operating on the very edge of Christendom. However, this is by no means the whole picture, for the Grail Knights in *Parsifal* also derive something from the Brahmanic and Buddhist traditions that occupied Wagner's thoughts for three decades.

The Brahmanic vision of society reflects a hierarchy of ritual 'purity' and a complex system of ritual and sacrifice. In that tradition, society comprises two groups: the descendants of nomadic people who came to India from ancient Iran early in the second millennium BC and spoke Old Indo-Aryan (that is, Sanskrit), and those who did not belong to this group. The former are divided into several hereditary classes in descending order of purity. The first class (the Brahmans) have a prerogative and duty to teach and maintain the religious tradition, the second class maintain order, and the third class generate wealth through farming and trade. The outsiders make up a fourth class whose basic duty is to serve the three other classes. This ideology of the ritual purity of the classes underpins the modern Indian caste system.

The Brahmans' hereditary status empowers them to carry out certain ritual functions from which members of other classes are excluded. In a sense, the Grail Knights with their rituals may be likened to the Brahmans; hence their obligatory knightly class status and preoccupation with purity, which entitles them to perform the functions of guardians of the Grail. Kundry, on the other hand, is one who serves the Knights, and describes herself as such. Her final (and only) words in Act Three are 'To serve – to serve'. She fetches and carries, brings medicine to Amfortas and water to Parsifal and, reluctantly, does Klingsor's bidding.

Her place in the Brahmanic class structure is clearly on the bottom rung.

On the other hand, the Buddha's teachings were formulated in contradiction of certain Brahmanic practices and flew in the face of the system of hereditary classes. The Buddha drew no distinction on grounds of race or class, attracted followers from all backgrounds and regarded all living beings as fellow sufferers in the endless cycle of existence. The way to salvation was open to all. Like the Buddha who had no qualms in offering salvation to the low-caste maiden Prakriti, in *Die Sieger*, so the Christian Parsifal has no qualms in offering salvation through baptism to the wretched and despised Kundry. Far from upholding a system based on exclusivity, Parsifal, the Innocent Fool, the outsider amongst the company of the Grail, establishes a new order based upon fellow suffering. He has won enlightenment through compassion, and it is for him that voices high up in the dome proclaim a benediction that also happens to be Wagner's farewell to the world:

'*Erlösung dem Erlöser*! – Redemption to the Redeemer!'

Libretto of Parsifal

A free translation of Wagner's text

CHARACTERS

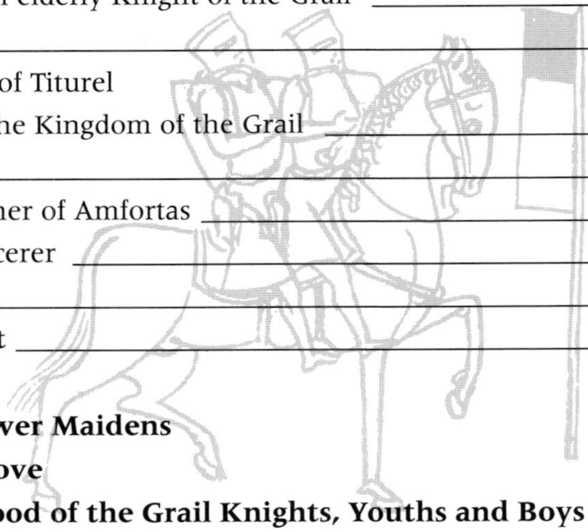

Gurnemanz, an elderly Knight of the Grail — *Bass*

Kundry — *Soprano*

Amfortas, son of Titurel
and ruler of the Kingdom of the Grail — *Baritone*

Parsifal — *Tenor*

Titurel, the father of Amfortas — *Bass*

Klingsor, a sorcerer — *Bass*

First Knight — *Tenor*

Second Knight — *Bass*

Four Squires

Klingsor's Flower Maidens

Voice from above

The Brotherhood of the Grail Knights, Youths and Boys

Scene of the Action

The domain and castle – 'Montsalvat' – of the Guardians of the Grail: scenery like that of the northern mountains of Gothic Spain. Later, Klingsor's enchanted castle on the southern slopes of the same mountains, facing Moorish Spain.

ACT ONE

A forest, shady and solemn but not gloomy. A clearing in the centre. A path leads upwards to the Grail Castle. The ground slopes away at the back to a lake. Daybreak. Gurnemanz, elderly but active, and two young squires lie sleeping. A solemn reveille rings out, as from the Grail castle.

Gurnemanz

You sleepy guardians of the woods, wake up to the morning. Do you hear the call? Give thanks to God that you hear it.

(He kneels with the squires, and together they offer up their morning prayer in silence.)

Now my boys, attend to the bath. I see heralds approaching ahead of the litter which bears the King.

(Two knights enter.)

Greetings! How is Amfortas today? He is early for his bath. I expect that the healing herb that Gawan found for him has brought relief?

Second Knight

His pain returned worse than before. After a sleepless night he was eager to take his bath.

Gurnemanz

We are fools to look for a cure in herbs and potions. Only one thing can help him, only one man!

Second Knight

Who is he?

Gurnemanz

(*evasively*) See to the bath.

Second Squire

Look, it is the 'wild rider'.

First Squire

See how the mane of her devil's mare is flying.

Second Knight

Is that Kundry?

First Knight

She must be bringing urgent news.

Second Squire

The mare stumbles.

First Squire

Has it been flying through the air?

Second Squire

It's down on the ground.

First Squire

It's mane is dragging through the moss.

Second Squire

The wild woman flings herself off.

(Kundry rushes in, almost staggering. She is in rough clothing. Her black hair is loose and dishevelled, her complexion a deep ruddy-brown, her eyes dark and piercing, sometimes flashing wildly, more often lifeless and staring. She hurries to Gurnemanz and presses into his hand a small phial.)

Kundry

Here! Take it! Balsam!

Gurnemanz

Where did you get this?

Kundry

From further away than you can imagine. If it does not cure him then there is nothing else to be found in Arabia. Ask nothing more of me.

(she throws herself down on the ground)

I am weary.

(A train of squires and knights appears carrying and escorting the litter on which lies Amfortas.)

Gurnemanz

They are carrying him here. I can not bear to see him, a proud and vigorous ruler struck down by this injury. Be careful, he is groaning.

(the squires halt and set down the litter)

Amfortas

(raising himself a little)

That will do. Thank you. A short rest in the splendour of the forest morning after a night of pain. The waters of the holy lake will refresh and soothe me. Gawan!

Second Knight

My lord, Gawan did not stay. When the herb which he won was of no use he sped away to continue his quest.

Amfortas

Without leave? He will have to atone for flaunting the Grail's command. Woe betide him if he falls into Klingsor's snares. Let no-one disturb my peace in this way. I shall wait for the appointed one: 'Enlightened through compassion', wasn't that it?

Gurnemanz

You told us so.

Amfortas

'The Innocent Fool'. I think I know him now: I would call him 'Death'!

Gurnemanz

(Giving Kundry's phial to Amfortas)

Try once more with this.

Amfortas

Where did this strange vessel come from?

Gurnemanz

It was brought for you from Arabia.

Amfortas

Who brought it?

Gurnemanz

There she lies, the wild woman. Get up Kundry! Come here!

(Kundry refuses and remains on the ground)

Amfortas

You Kundry. Must I thank you once again, you shy and restless maid? Very well, I'll try this balsam as thanks for your loyalty.

Kundry

Don't thank me! What help will it be? Away to your bath.

(Amfortas gives the signal to move on. Kundry remains on the ground. Squires come and go.)

Third Squire

Hey, you there! Why do you lie there like a wild beast.

Kundry

Aren't the beasts sacred here?

Third Squire

Yes, but we don't know whether you are sacred!

Fourth Squire

She will finish off our master with her magic potion.

Gurnemanz

Has she ever harmed you? When you can't think of a way of sending messages to our brothers fighting in far off lands, who rushes there and back for us? You don't support her and she never looks to you for anything. Yet when help is wanted in times of danger she rushes away and never looks for thanks. If this amounts to harm, then it works out well for you.

Third Squire

But she hates us. Just see how she glares at us.

Fourth Squire

She's a heathen, a sorceress.

Gurnemanz

She may be cursed. She lives here now, perhaps reincarnated, to atone for some guilt in a former life. Now she makes atonement by helping our knightly order. She has done well, serving us and thereby helping herself.

Third Squire

Perhaps it was this guilt of hers that brought such trouble upon us?

Gurnemanz

Perhaps. When she was away from us for a long time, misfortune did befall us. I have known her a long time but Titurel has known her longer. When he was building the castle he found her asleep in the undergrowth, as if dead. I found her again that way after that evildoer beyond the mountains brought such misfortune and shame upon us.

(to Kundry)

Tell us, where were you roaming when our master lost the Spear?

(Kundry is gloomily silent)

Why didn't you help us then?

Kundry

I never help.

Fourth Squire

There, she said it.

Third Squire

If she is so daring, then send her after the missing Spear!

Gurnemanz

That is a different matter. It is forbidden to all.

O wondrous, hallowed Spear, I saw thee wielded by unholiest hand. Valiant Amfortas, who could have prevented you from defeating the sorcerer?

Near the keep the hero was enticed away; a woman of great beauty bewitched him. He lay intoxicated in her arms and let the Spear fall. There was a deathly cry and I rushed in. Klingsor, laughing, was making his escape with the Holy Spear. A wound burned in the King's side that will never heal.

Third Squire

(to Gurnemanz)

Then you knew Klingsor?

Gurnemanz

(to the two returning squires)

How is the King?

First Squire

The bath has refreshed him.

Second Squire

The balsam eased his pain.

Gurnemanz

(to himself)

The wound that will never heal.

Third Squire

But father tell us, you knew Klingsor – how could that be?

Gurnemanz

Titurel, the godly hero knew him well. At a time when the realm of the true faith was threatened, the Saviour's angel messengers came from heaven bearing the sacred vessel from which he drank at the last meal of love, and into which his divine blood had flowed from the Cross. With this was also brought the Spear which had shed his blood. They gave these treasures into the charge of our King, and for them he built this sanctuary. You know that only the pure may become one of the brothers, to whom the Grail grants the strength to work divine salvation. This was forbidden to Klingsor, although he spent much effort on it. He lived in the distant valley, beyond which lies a rich heathen land. I never knew of what sin he was guilty, but he wished to atone and become sanctified.

Unable to suppress the sin within him, he turned violent hands upon himself, which he then offered to the Grail. The guardian scornfully turned him away. Klingsor's fury taught him how his act of ignoble sacrifice could lead to evil sorcery. He transformed the desert into a garden of bliss in which bloomed women of devilish beauty. Now he lures the knights into sinful joys and hell's damnation. Many have already succumbed. When Titurel in old age had conferred the kingship on his son, Amfortas could not wait to subdue this sorcery. You know what happened; the Spear is now in Klingsor's hands, and he imagines that the Grail is already his.

(Kundry has been turning back and forth, greatly agitated)

Fourth Squire

More than anything else, the Spear must be ours again.

Third Squire

Ha! He who brings it back would win fame and glory.

Gurnemanz

Amfortas lay before the robbed sanctuary in fervent prayer for some sign of salvation. Amidst a blessed radiance from the Grail, in a holy vision he saw the shining words: 'Enlightened through compassion, the innocent fool; wait for him the appointed one.'

The Four Squires

(deeply moved)

'Enlightened through compassion, the innocent fool ...'

(From the lake come shouts and cries from the knights and squires. Gurnemanz and the four squires start up in alarm.)

Knights and Squires

Alas! Alas! Who caused this outrage?
A wild swan. It's wounded.

(A wild swan flutters injured from over the lake.)

Gurnemanz

Who shot the swan?

(The swan falls to the ground exhausted. The Second Knight draws an arrow from its breast.)

First Knight

The King greeted it as a happy omen when the swan circled over the lake, and then an arrow flew …

(Knights and Squires lead Parsifal in.)

Knights

He is the one. His the shot. His the bow.

Second Knight

Here is the arrow, just like his.

Gurnemanz

(to Parsifal)

Are you the one who killed this swan?

Parsifal

Indeed! Whatever flies I can hit in flight!

Gurnemanz

You did this, and you are not concerned by it?

Squires and Knights

Punish the offender.

Gurnemanz

You could murder here in this holy forest? Didn't the woodland beasts tamely come near you and innocently greet you as friends? What did the birds sing to you from the branches? What harm did that faithful swan do you? Seeking its mate, it circled the lake and sanctified the King's bath. Didn't you wonder at it? Were you just tempted to a childish shot from your bow? He delighted us. What is he now to you? Here

– look – here you struck him, the blood is still congealing, the wings drooping lifeless. The snowy plumage is stained dark, the eyes glazed – do you see the look?

(Parsifal has followed Gurnemanz with growing emotion. He breaks his bow and hurls away his arrows.)

Do you understand what you have done? How could you do it?

Parsifal

I didn't know.

Gurnemanz

Where are you from?

Parsifal

I don't know.

Gurnemanz

Who is your father?

Parsifal

I don't know.

Gurnemanz

Who sent you this way?

Parsifal

I don't know.

Gurnemanz

Your name then?

Parsifal

I had many, but I no longer know them.

Gurnemanz

You know nothing of anything?
I have never met such a dullard before – except Kundry.

(to the squires, who have assembled in increasing numbers)

Now go! Do not neglect the King's bath! Help here!

(The squires reverently lift the dead swan onto a litter of fresh branches and leave with it towards the lake.)

Now, you know nothing of what I ask you. Tell me what you do know.

Parsifal

I have a mother whose name is Herzeleide. Our home was in the woods and wild moors.

Gurnemanz

Who gave you the bow?

Parsifal

I made it myself to chase the wild eagles from the forest.

Gurnemanz

But you appear eagle-like and nobly born. Why didn't your mother have you taught better weapons?

(Parsifal is silent.)

Kundry

(following Parsifal keenly, she calls out roughly)

His mother bore him fatherless, when Gamuret was slain in battle! To save her son from a similar fate she raised him in the wilderness, ignorant of arms, as a fool – as fool she was!

(she laughs)

Parsifal

Yes! And once by the forest's edge came glittering men mounted on fine animals. I wanted to be like them. They laughed and rode away. I ran after them but could not overtake them. I travelled through desert and hill and valley, night and day, with my bow to protect me against wild beasts and giants.

Kundry

Yes! Robbers and giants tested his strength. They learned to fear him.

Parsifal

(in surprise)

Who fears me?

Kundry

The wicked.

Parsifal

They who attacked me, were they wicked?

(Gurnemanz laughs)

Who is good?

Gurnemanz

Your mother whom you deserted, and now she worries and grieves for you.

Kundry

She grieves no more: his mother is dead.

Parsifal

(in great alarm)

Dead? My mother? Who says so?

Kundry

As I rode by I saw her dying. She bade me greet you, fool.

(Parsifal springs furiously at Kundry and seizes her by the throat. Gurnemanz restrains him.)

Parsifal

Are you mad, boy! More violence? What harm has she done you? She spoke the truth, for Kundry never lies, although she has seen much.

Parsifal

(Seized with violent trembling)

I feel faint!

(Kundry hastens to a spring in the wood and brings water, sprinkles Parsifal with it and gives it to him to drink.)

Gurnemanz

Well done! That accords well with the Grail's mercy. Whoever repays ill with good overcomes it.

Kundry

I never do good. All I want is rest. I am so weary.
To sleep! O that none should wake me!

(starting in fear)

No! Not sleep! Terror seizes me!
But sleep I must.

(She sinks down behind the bushes.)

Gurnemanz

The King is returning from his bath; the sun is high. Now let me lead you to our hallowed feast; for if you are pure the Grail will give you food and drink.

Parsifal

Who is the Grail?

Gurnemanz

That cannot be said, but if you are called to its service that knowledge will not be held from you. No earthly path leads to it and none could tread it whom the Grail has not guided.

Parsifal

I scarcely tread yet already seem to have come far.

Gurnemanz

You see, my son, here time becomes space.

(While they slowly walk, the woods disappear, and in the rocky walls a gateway appears, through which they pass. The way leads upwards through the rock. There is a sound of bells, swelling and dying. The scene has entirely changed, and they enter the mighty hall of the castle of the Grail.

Gurnemanz

Now note well, and let me see, if you are a fool and innocent, what knowledge may be granted to you.

(The scene is a pillared hall, with a cupola over the refectory. Knights of the Grail enter and arrange themselves at the tables.)

Knights of the Grail

At this last Meal of Love prepared day by day.

(A procession of squires passes rapidly across the scene into the background.)

As at the Last Supper, may it refresh us today.

(A second procession of squires crosses the hall.)

The meal will be renewed for him who delights in doing good. Let him draw near and receive the highest gift.

(Amfortas is carried in on a litter and set down on a raised couch. Before it is the shrine of the Grail.)

Youths

(From half-way up in the dome)

As for the sinful world, with a thousand pains His blood once flowed, now with a joyful heart let my blood be shed for the Redeemer. The body He gave to purge our sin lives on in us through His death.

Boys

(From the highest point in the dome)

The faith lives; the dove soars, the Saviour's fairest messenger. Drink the wine poured out for you and take the bread of life!

(When all have taken their places, and after a complete silence, the voice of Titurel is heard in the far background from a vaulted niche behind Amfortas, as if from a tomb.)

Titurel

Amfortas, my son, are you in your place? Shall I again today look on the Grail and live? Must I die without my Saviour's guidance?

Amfortas

Woe! Woe for my pain!
My father, once more perform this duty yourself! Live, live – and let me die!

Titurel

Within the grave I live by the Saviour's grace, but I am too weak to serve him. In his service you may expiate your sin! – Uncover the Grail!

Amfortas

No! Leave it covered! Oh, no one must know the torment that this sight arouses in me, and yet delights you! What is the wound's pain compared with the hellish pangs of being condemned to this office! Woeful is the inheritance to which I am called – the only sinner amongst all my people – to tend the Holy of Holies. Oh punishment of the wronged Lord of mercy! I must long for Him and His sacred greeting. I must reach out to Him from the penance of my soul. The hour draws near. A ray of light descends on the holy relic. The covering falls. The divine liquid of the sacred cup glows with brilliant power. Thrilled by the pangs of joy, I feel the holiest blood flow into my heart. My own sinful blood surging wildly must flow back to me and gush into the world of sinful lust. Anew it streams out through the wound inflicted by the same thrust which opened the Redeemer's wound. With tears of blood, the Divine One wept with pity over man's disgrace. Now from me, the custodian of the godliest treasures, wells my sinful blood, ever stirred by yearning and never staunched by repentance. Have mercy! Have mercy! Take my heritage and heal the wound, so that I may die holy and pure in Thee!

Boys and Youths

'Enlightened through compassion, the innocent fool: Wait for him, the chosen one!'

Knights

Thus it was promised. Wait with confidence. Perform your duty today.

Titurel

Uncover the Grail.

(Amfortas raises himself slowly and painfully. The Grail is uncovered before Amfortas.)

Voices

'Take this my Body, take this my Blood, in token of our love!'

Boys

'Take this my Blood, take this my Body, in remembrance of me!'

Titurel

Oh! heavenly joy, how brightly our Lord greets this day!

(The Grail is covered again.)

Boys

Wine and bread of that Last Supper were once changed by the Lord of the Grail through compassionate love, to the Blood which He shed and the Body which He gave.

(The bread and wine are now distributed to the knights, including Gurnemanz, who keeps a seat vacant next to him and gestures to Parsifal to take part in the meal. However, Parsifal remains standing motionless.)

Youths

Blood and Body of the holy gift now refreshes you, turning through loving consolation into the wine poured out for you and to the bread given to you to eat.

Knights

Take of the bread, turn it boldly into the body's power and strength, true to death, steadfast in labour, to do the Saviour's works! Take of the wine, turn it anew into the fiery blood of life, gladly united in brotherly faith to fight with holy courage.

Knights, Youths and Boys

Blessed in faith and love! Blessed in faith!

(Amfortas holds his hand to the wound which bleeds afresh. He is borne away. The knights form a solemn procession and leave the hall. The doors are closed. Parsifal still stands unmoving.)

Gurnemanz

(approaching Parsifal and shaking his arm)

Are you still here? Do you know what you have seen?

(Parsifal clutches his heart and slightly shakes his head)

You are nothing but a fool!

(opens a narrow side door)

Off with you, on your way! But heed Gurnemanz: in future leave the swans in peace! A gander should look for a goose!

(He pushes Parsifal out and slams the door behind him.)

A Voice

'Enlightened through compassion, the innocent fool.'

Voices

Blessed in faith!

ACT TWO

Klingsor's magic castle. The inner keep of a tower open to the sky. Stone steps lead to the battlements on the tower wall. The stage represents the projecting wall of the tower, which leads down into darkness below. Implements of witchcraft and necromantic apparatus. Klingsor on the projecting wall, to one side, sitting before a metal mirror.

Klingsor

The time has come. My magic castle lures the fool who approaches from afar with childish exuberance. My curse holds the woman fast in a grip only I can loosen. Up then! To work!

(He calls into the darkness below with mysterious gestures)

Arise! Arise! To me! Your master calls you, nameless one, She-devil of old! Rose of Hell! Herodias you were – and what besides? Gundryggia there, Kundry here! Come here! Here, I say! Kundry! Your master calls: arise!

(Kundry's shape arises in the bluish light. She seems asleep. Gradually however she moves like one awakening. Finally she utters a terrible scream.)

Are you awake? Ha! You have fallen under my spell again today at the right time. Tell me, where have you been roaming again? Fie! Among the knights where they treat you like a beast! Don't you fare better with me? When you captured their master for me – ha, ha, that chaste guardian of the Grail! What drove you forth again?

Kundry

(hoarsely and brokenly, as if trying to regain speech)

Oh! Oh! Deepest night! Frenzy! O rage! O misery! Sleep … sleep … deep sleep! … death!

Klingsor

You have awoken, eh?

Kundry

Yes … my curse! O yearning … yearning!

Klingsor

Haha, for those saintly knights?

Kundry

There … there … I served.

Klingsor

Yes – to make good the wrong you had maliciously done them? They won't help, venal as they are, if I bid the right price. The strongest will fall when he sinks into your arms and so be brought low by the Spear which I seized from their master. Now today we have the most dangerous to meet; the shield of foolishness protects him.

Kundry

I … will not … Oh! … Oh!

Klingsor

You will, because you must.

Kundry

You … cannot … force me.

Klingsor

But I can hold you.

Kundry

You?

Klingsor

Your master.

Kundry

By what power?

Klingsor

Because only against me is your power useless.

Kundry

(laughing shrilly)

Ha ha! Are you chaste?

Klingsor

(furiously)

Why do you ask this accursed witch? What a terrible fate. Now the fiend mocks me because I once strove after holiness? The torture of unbridled desire, most hellish impulse which I had stifled into deathly silence – does it now laugh aloud and mock me through you, bride of the devil? Beware! Already one pays for his scorn and contempt, that proud man, strong in holiness who once drove me out. I ruined his race. The guardian of the holy treasure will languish unredeemed, and soon – I know it – I shall guard the Grail myself. Ha Ha! How did you like the hero Amfortas whom I ensnared for you?

Kundry

Oh! Anguish! ... Anguish! He too was weak. They are all weak who fall victim to my curse! O eternal sleep, the only salvation, how can I win you?

Klingsor

Ha! He that defies you will set you free: try it on the boy who approaches!

Kundry

I will not!

Klingsor

Already he is climbing the stronghold.

Kundry

Alas! Alas! Did I wake for this? Must I? Must I?

Klingsor

Ha! The boy is handsome!

Kundry

O! Woe is me!

Klingsor

Ho, guards! Ho. knights! Enemies are at hand! Ha! How they rush to the ramparts, my deluded garrison, to defend their beautiful witches! So! Courage! Courage! Ha! He doesn't fear them. He has seized the sword of the warrior Ferris and wields it mightily against the throng. How poorly the others fare! He has slashed one in the arm, another in the thigh. Aha! They give way.

(Kundry vanishes)

They flee! Each has a wound to carry home! They are welcome to them. May the whole breed of knights slaughter each other! Ha! How proudly he stands on the ramparts! How the roses in his cheeks bloom, and he stares at the sight of the garden! Hey! Kundry! What? Already at work? Haha! I chose well the spell which summons you to my service! You there, childish boy, whatever the prophesies say, too young and foolish, you fall into my power. Once striped of your purity you will remain my slave!

(He sinks rapidly with the whole tower: immediately the magic garden rises and fills the whole stage. Tropical vegetation; luxuriant display of flowers. Towards the rear, the scene is bounded by the battlements of the castle walls, in a rich Arabian style with terraces. Parsifal stands on the rampart, gazing down into the garden with astonishment. From all sides lovely maidens rush in, singly and then in groups. They are dressed in veils of soft colours, hastily draped as if they have been startled from sleep.)

Flower Maidens

Here! The noise came from here! Weapons – wild cries. Who is the evil one? Revenge! My beloved was wounded! I woke alone! Where is my beloved? Where are our lovers? We saw their wounds bleeding. There he stands! What a disaster! Accursed you shall be!

(Parsifal leaps down into the garden)

Ha! You are bold! How dare you approach? Why did you strike our lovers?

Parsifal

You lovely children, wasn't I forced to strike them? They barred my way to you pretty ones.

Flower Maidens

You wanted to reach us? Have you seen us before?

Parsifal

I have never seen such a pretty group; is it fitting to call you beautiful?

Flower Maidens

Then you won't strike us?

Parsifal

I would never do that.

Flower Maidens

You have injured our playmates. Who will play with us now?

Parsifal

I'll do that gladly.

(The girls burst into laughter. One group slips way to complete their flowery garb.)

Flower Maidens

If you are our friend, don't go far away and we shall make it up to you. We don't play for gold, we play for love's reward.

(The first group return having completed their dressing and throw themselves on Parsifal.)

Leave the boy! He's mine! No, mine!

Other Flower Maidens

Oh how cunning, they dressed in secret!

(The remainder of the girls leave to dress themselves.)

Come, come, handsome boy! Let me bloom for you, to please and refresh you will be my labour of love!

Parsifal

How sweet you smell. Are you flowers then?

Flower Maidens

The jewels of the garden, fragrant spirits, plucked in the Spring by our master! Hear we grow beneath the Summer sun, happily blooming for you, so be kind and gentle with us! Let me blossom for you! Let me cool your brow! Let me touch your cheeks! Let me kiss your lips! No! I am the fairest! No! I am the fairest! My fragrance is sweeter!

Parsifal

You wild throng of lovely flowers, If I am to play with you, give me some room!

Flower Maidens

Why struggle?

Parsifal

Because you quarrel.

Flower Maidens

We quarrel over you.

Parsifal

Then don't.

Flower Maidens

Let him go! See he wants me! No! He wants me! Would you have the flowers woo the butterfly? How cold he is, how hesitant! Away! Let's leave the fool! We give him up, yet he is our chosen one! No ours! No ours!

Parsifal

Leave me! You'll not trap me!

Kundry

Parsifal! Stay!

Parsifal

Parsifal? My mother called me that once in a dream.

(The girls start at the sound of Kundry's voice and immediately leave Parsifal.)

Kundry

Stay, Parsifal! Bliss and happiness together greet you. Childish flirts, leave him alone. Flowers soon fade, he was not meant for your games. Go home tend the wounded; many lonely knights await you.

Flower Maidens

Leave you! Avoid you! Willingly we'd forsake all others to be alone with you. Farewell fair and proud fool!

(The girls disappear laughing into the castle. There appears a young woman of great beauty – Kundry, in an entirely different form – lying on a bed of flowers, dressed in a revealing, fanciful garment.

Parsifal

Have I dreamt this? Did you call me, who have no name?

Kundry

I named you, foolish pure one, 'Falparsi'; you pure fool, 'Parsifal'. Thus your father Gamuret called to his son as he died in an Arabian land, greeting him still in his mother's womb. I am here to tell you this. What else could have brought you here, other than a wish to know?

Parsifal

I have never before imagined what I am seeing now, and it frightens me. Did you too bloom in this grove of flowers?

Kundry

No, Parsifal foolish and pure! My home is far away. I have only waited here so you could find me. I have come from far off and I have seen much. I have seen the child at his mother's breast. Even with sorrow in her heart, Herzeleide laughed with your childish sounds. Her greatest concern was to protect you against the perils which your father had known. She hoped to hide and shelter you in peace, far from arms and the fury of warriors. Can't you still hear the cry of her lament when you lingered far away from her? Oh! what joy it gave her to find you. When she clasped you firmly, weren't you frightened by her kisses? But you didn't see her grief when, finally, you did not return and all trace of you was lost. She waited day and night, until her wailing ceased. Her grief overwhelmed even the pain, and she sought a silent death. Sorrow broke her heart – and Heart's Sorrow died.

Parsifal

(Sinks shocked, and overcome with grief at Kundry's feet.)

Alas! What have I done? Where was I? Mother! Sweet, gentle mother! Your son, your son has to be your murderer! O fool! Stupid, blundering fool! Where were you roaming oblivious to you, dearest, beloved mother!

Kundry

Have you never known how being comforted can take away your pain? This calamity, this distress can be removed through the comfort of love.

Parsifal

My mother, how could I forget you! Oh, what else have I forgotten? What have I ever remembered? Foolishness alone lives within me.

Kundry

Confession will put an end to guilt and remorse, and knowledge will turn folly into sense. Learn to know the love that was Gamuret's when Herzeleide's searing passion held him! She who gave you life offers you today this last greeting of a mother's blessing, the first kiss of love!

(She presses her lips to his in a long kiss. Parsifal suddenly starts up with a gesture of extreme fear: he clutches at his heart as if to contain some rending pain.)

Parsifal

Amfortas! The wound! The wound! It burns in my side! A terrible wailing cries from the depths of my heart. Oh wretch most miserable! The wound I saw bleeding now bleeds in me! Here – here! No! It is not the wound. May its blood pour forth in streams! Here! The flame in my heart! The longing, the terrible longing that seizes all my being! Oh torment of love! How everything trembles, quakes and quivers in sinful desire! My gaze is fixed upon the holy vessel; the holy blood glows. Redemption's bliss excites every soul. Only here in my heart will torment fail to be stilled. I hear the Saviour's lamentation, ah! the lamentation from his defiled sanctuary: 'Redeem me, rescue me from guilt-stained hands!' And I, the fool and coward, I fled here to wild and childish deeds!

(Despairing, he throws himself on his knees.)

Redeemer! Saviour! Lord of Grace! How may I, sinner, erase my guilt?

Kundry

Worthy hero, throw off this spell and greet the fair one who comes to you!

Parsifal

(still kneeling, gazes at Kundry who bends over him with caresses)

Yes, this was the voice with which she called him, this her look which I recognise, her disturbing laughter, her bending neck, her boldly tossed head and fluttering tresses. Thus she slipped her arm around his neck and gently caressed his cheek. Harnessing every torment, her mouth kissed away the salvation of his soul! Ha! this kiss! Destroyer! Away from me! For ever! Ever from me!

Kundry

Cruel! If you are conscious only of the sufferings of others then feel mine! If you are a redeemer, what stops you from uniting us in salvation? For eternities I've watched for you, the Saviour come so late! Whom once I dared to scorn. Oh, if you but knew the curse that racks me in sleep and waking, death and night, pain and laughter and prepares me for new sorrows. I saw Him – Him – and laughed … . Then his glance fell on me! Now from world to world I seek him, to meet him once again. His gaze rests on me, and then that accursed laugh returns: a sinner sinks into my arms! Then I laugh and laugh and cannot weep, but only shriek and rage and storm in an ever-recurring nightmare from which I rarely wake. Let me weep upon the breast of him for whom I yearned, the foolish and the scorned. Let me spend but one hour with you, and though God and the world reject me, be absolved and redeemed!

Parsifal

For all eternity you would be damned with me if I were to forget my mission for only an hour in your embrace! I am sent for your salvation too, if you will turn from desire. The cleansing of your soul comes not from the source from which your suffering flows. Salvation shall never be yours until that source dries up within you. I saw the brothers in terrible need, tormenting themselves. But who can know with certainty the true source of salvation? Oh the darkness of worldly error that while earnestly seeking salvation, men thirst for the fountain of damnation!

Kundry

Was it my kiss that revealed the world to you? The full embrace of my love then would raise you to godhead. Redeem the world if this is your destiny; make yourself a god for an hour; and let me be damned forever, my wound never to be healed!

Parsifal

Redemption I offer you as well.

Kundry

Let me love you godly one, and you would then give me redemption.

Parsifal

Love and redemption shall be yours if you will show me the way to Amfortas.

Kundry

(furiously)

You shall never find him! He has fallen; let him perish, that wretch seeking after shame, whom I scorned with laughter! Haha! He fell by his own spear!

Parsifal

Who dared to wound him with the holy weapon?

Kundry

He who once punished my laughter; his curse gives me strength. Against even you I'll call the Spear if you offer pity to that sinner. Ha! Madness! Pity me instead, and let one hour be mine! For one hour let me be yours and you shall be shown the way.

(She tries to embrace him but he thrusts her violently away.)

Parsifal

Away, evil woman!

Kundry

Help! Help! Here! Seize the wretch! Bar his way! And though you flee from here and find all the roads of the world, that road you seek most you shall not find. I curse any path that leads you away from me. You on whom I depend, I give him into your power!

(Klingsor has appeared on the battlements and brandishes a spear at Parsifal.)

Klingsor

Stop! I have just the weapon for you! The fool shall fall to me through his master's spear!

(He hurls the Spear, which remains poised above Parsifal's head.)

Parsifal

(Seizing the Spear and holding it above his head)

With this sign I banish your magic, just as it will heal the wound you caused with it, and destroy your hollow power!

(He swings the Spear in the sign of the Cross. The castle sinks as if by an earthquake and the garden shrivels to a desert. Kundry falls to the ground with a scream. Parsifal pauses at the top of a ruined wall and turns back to Kundry.)

Parsifal

You know where you can find me again!

(He hurries away. Kundry raise her head a little and gazes after him.)

ACT THREE

In the domain of the Grail. A pleasant open Spring landscape with a background of gently rising flowery meadows. The edge of the forest forms the foreground. By the side of the wood is a spring; facing it, a little further back, is a humble hermit's hut. Very early morning. Gurnemanz, now a very old man, clad as a hermit and only in the tunic of the Knights of the Grail, comes out of the hut and listens.

Gurnemanz

The groaning came from over there. No beast makes such a sound, especially on this, the holiest of mornings.

(Hollow groaning of Kundry's voice.)

I think I know this lamentation.

(He wrenches the bushes apart)

Ha! She is here again? The rough wintry thorns have kept her hidden – how long I wonder? Up! Kundry! Up! Awake to Spring! Cold and stiff! I would think her dead but I heard her groan.

(Gurnemanz rubs Kundry's hands and temples vigorously. A last she awakens. Kundry is in the coarse robe of a penitent. She looks much as she did in Act One but her face is paler and the wildness has vanished from her looks and behaviour. She gazes long at Gurnemanz and then rises, arranges her clothing and hair and sets to work like a serving maid.)

You crazy woman, have you no word to thank me for having woken you from a deathly sleep?

Kundry

To serve … to serve!

Gurnemanz

(shaking his head)

There is little work for you. We send out no more messages, and each finds herbs and roots for himself. We have learned this in the forest from the beasts.

(Kundry goes inside the hut.)

She moves so differently. Has the holy day brought this about? O day of mercy; it was for her salvation that I was able to rouse her.

(Kundry returns carrying a water pitcher and goes with it to the spring. She notices someone coming from the distance and points this out to Gurnemanz. Kundry moves away with the filled pitcher into the hut.)

Who is this approaching the holy spring in solemn armour? It is not one of the brothers.

(Parsifal emerges from the forest wearing black armour with closed visor, and carrying a lowered spear. He moves hesitantly and seats himself on a small grassy mound by the spring. Gurnemanz draws near to him.)

Greetings, guest! Have you lost your way, and may I direct you?

(Parsifal gently shakes his head)

Do you offer me no greeting?

(Parsifal bows his head)

If you vows prevent you from speaking, then mine require me to tell you what is fitting. here you are in a hallowed place. No man comes here armed, especially today of all days. Do you know what day it is?

(Parsifal shakes his head.)

No? Then where do you come from? It must have been amongst the heathen not to have known that today is the supremely holy Good Friday? Lay down your weapons. Do not offend the Lord, who today, bereft of all arms, offered his holy blood to redeem the sinful world.

(Parsifal slowly rises, thrusts the Spear into the ground, opens his helmet and lays it on the ground with his other weapons. He then kneels before the Spear in silent prayer. Gurnemanz watches with astonishment and emotion, and beckons to Kundry, who has emerged from the hut.)

Do you recognise him? It is he who once killed the swan.

(Kundry gives a slight nod of her head)

It is indeed the fool whom I drove away in anger. How did he find his way? Ah, the Spear, I recognise it! O most holy day, that I should wake to see it!

(Parsifal rises slowly from prayer. He recognises Gurnemanz and gently offers his hand in greeting.)

Parsifal

I rejoice to have found you again.

Gurnemanz

Then you recognise me, though grief and care have bowed me low? How have you come now, and from where?

Parsifal

I have travelled the path of error and suffering. Am I freed from it now that I hear again the murmur of the forest and greet you again? Everything seems changed.

Gurnemanz

Whom were you seeking?

Parsifal

He whose lament I once heard in foolish wonder. I believe myself ordained to bring him salvation. An evil curse drove me on trackless wanderings and dangers, battles and conflicts led me from my path. I received many wounds, for this Spear I dared not use in battle. I have now brought it home, undefiled – the Grail's holy Spear.

Gurnemanz

O sublime happiness! O sublime miracle!

(to Parsifal)

Oh Sir! If a curse drove you from the true path, believe me, it has lifted. You are in the land of the Grail and its knights await you. They have need of the consolation that you bring. From the day that you were here, our grief and distress has grown. Amfortas longs for death because of the torment of his wound. No plea can move him to perform his holy office and the Grail remains locked in its shrine, for he cannot die while he still looks upon it. The holy bread is now denied us and we make do with common food. Our heroes' strength is exhausted, and our dispirited and leaderless knights wander about. I live in a corner of the forest, awaiting that death to which the aged, warrior lord surrendered. Titurel, deprived the sight of the Grail, is dead – a man like all men!

Parsifal

(springing up in intense grief)

And it is I who caused all this misery. Ah! what transgression, what burden of guilt must my foolish head have borne from eternity, since no repentance, no atonement can free me from my blindness. Though I was chosen for deliverance, the last path of deliverance is lost for me.

(Parsifal seems about to fall in a faint. Gurnemanz assists him to the grassy mound and Kundry hurriedly fetches a bowl of water.)

Gurnemanz

(gently repulsing Kundry)

Not that! – The holy spring itself will refresh our pilgrim. I suspect that today he has to perform important work, a holy office. Now let the stain and dust of his wanderings be washed from him.

(Gurnemanz and Kundry gently lead Parsifal to the edge of the spring and loosen his armour.)

Parsifal

Shall I see Amfortas?

Gurnemanz

Certainly; the great castle awaits us and the solemn funeral rites of my dear lord summon me there. Amfortas has promised that he will once again reveal to us the Grail, to sanctify his noble father, slain by his son's misdeed. Thus he will atone.

(Kundry bathes Parsifal's feet with humility. Parsifal watches her in silent wonder.)

Parsifal

You wash my feet. Now bathe my head, oh friend!

Gurnemanz

(scooping his hand in the spring and sprinkling Parsifal's head)

My this purity bless you, pure one! Thus may the load of all guilt be washed away!

(While Gurnemanz solemnly sprinkles the water, Kundry draws from her bosom a golden phial and pours part of its contents over Parsifal's feet, which she then dries with her hastily unbound hair.)

Parsifal

(gently taking the phial from Kundry and handing it to Gurnemanz)

You have anointed my feet. Let Titurel's knight anoint my head and greet me today as king!

(Gurnemanz empties the phial over Parsifal's head and lays his hands upon it.)

Gurnemanz

So it was promised, and so my blessings on your head, that I may greet you as king.

You so pure, compassionately enduring. As you have endured the sufferings of the redeemed, lift the final burden from his head.

(Parsifal scoops up water from the spring.)

Parsifal

My first duty I thus perform.

(He bends over Kundry, still kneeling before him, and sprinkles her head.)

Receive this baptism, and believe in the Redeemer!

(Kundry bows her head to the ground and appears to be weeping bitterly. Parsifal gazes on the wood and meadow, which are now glowing in the morning light.)

How very beautiful the meadow seems today. Once I came upon magic flowers which twined their tainted tendrils about my head. But I have never seen the grass and flowers so fresh and charming, nor smell so sweet and child-like, nor speak with such tender love to me.

Gurnemanz

That is the magic of Good Friday, my lord!

Parsifal

For such a day of utmost grief I could imagine that all that blooms, lives and lives anew should only mourn and weep.

Gurnemanz

You can see that this is not so. The tears of repentant sinners sprinkle the meadow with holy dew, and now all nature rejoices at the Saviour's sign of love. It no longer sees Him on the Cross, but man redeemed, freed of the burden of sin and terror through God's loving sacrifice. The grasses and flowers of the meadow know that today the foot of man will not tread them down, just as God with divine patience pitied mankind. Thus all creation gives thanks for all that here blooms and soon fades, now that nature, absolved from sin, today gains its day of innocence.

Parsifal

I saw those who once mocked me wither: do they long for redemption today?

(Kundry looks up at Parsifal with tearful eyes in calm and earnest entreaty.)

Your tears too become a dew of blessing: you weep – and see, the meadow smiles!

(He kisses her gently on the forehead. A peal of bells is heard in the distance.)

Gurnemanz

Midday. The hour has come. Permit your servant, lord, to guide you.

(Parsifal solemnly takes up the Spear and, with Kundry, follows Gurnemanz. The scene gradually changes, as in Act One. After remaining visible for a while, the three disappear completely from sight as the forest gradually vanishes and cliffs take its place. In the vaulted passages, the sound of bells grows in intensity. The walls open and disclose again the great hall of the Grail, but without the tables. From one side, knights enter bearing Titurel's body in a coffin; from the other those carrying Amfortas on a litter.)

1st Procession of Knights

(with Amfortas)

We carry in its shrine the Grail to its holy office. Whom have you that you bear in that gloomy shrine?

2nd Procession of Knights

(as they pass one another)

This funeral shrine holds the warrior into whose care God once gave Himself; Titurel we bear.

1st Procession

Who slew him, that once God himself protected?

2nd Procession

The burden of age when he no longer beheld the Grail.

1st Procession

Who denied him the sight of the Grail's favour?

2nd Procession

The guilty guardian, whom you bear.

1st Procession

We bear him today, for this last time he will perform his office.

(Amfortas is set down on the couch behind the Grail table, and the coffin before it.)

Knights

Woe, guardian of the Grail. For the last time be mindful of your duty! For the last time!

Amfortas

Woe! I freely cry with you, but more freely would I accept death from you, the mildest atonement for sin.

(The coffin is opened. At the sight of Titurel's corpse, all break into a sudden wailing.)

Amfortas

My father! Most blessed of warriors! Purest of all before whom the angels once bowed. Desiring only to die myself, I gave you death! Implore of the Saviour to grant the brothers new life while granting me death at last! To die – the only grace. Close the terrible wound, the poison that stiffens the heart! My father, I call to you; call to Him, 'Redeemer, give my son peace!'

Knights

Reveal the Grail! Perform your duty! Your father exhorts you. You must! You must!

(Amfortas hurls himself into the midst of the knights)

Amfortas

No! No more! I feel death already closing around me; should I then return to life? Madmen! Who shall compel me to live? But you could give me death!

(He tears open his robe)

Hear I am, and here is the open wound! Take out your weapons and thrust them deep to the hilt! Slay the sinner and his torment and then the Grail shall glow by itself for you!

(Unobserved by the knights, Parsifal has appeared among them. He now steps forward and stretches out the Spear and touches Amfortas' wound with its tip.)

Parsifal

One weapon will suffice – the wound is healed by the Spear that caused it. You are whole and have atoned! I now shall perform your task. Blessed be your suffering that gave compassion and wisdom to the timid fool!

(Parsifal holds the Spear on high.)

I bring back to you the holy Spear! This that heals your wound I see running with holy blood, yearning for that kindred source that flows in the depth of the Grail. No more shall it be hidden – open the shrine!

(Parsifal sinks to his knees in silent prayer before the Grail, which glows with a soft light.)

Boys, Youths and Knights

(with barely audible voices from the centre and apex of the dome)

Highest, holy miracle! Redemption to the Redeemer!

A beam of light falls on the Grail, which glows brightly. From the dome a white dove descends and hovers over Parsifal's head. Kundry slowly sinks lifeless to the ground in front of Parsifal, her eyes uplifted to him. Amfortas and Gurnemanz kneel in homage, as Parsifal offers the Grail's benediction to the worshipping knights.

Significant dates

1813	Wilhelm Richard Wagner born in Leipzig on 22 May. Father dies.
1814	Family moves to Dresden.
1821	Stepfather Ludwig Geyer dies.
1827	Returns with family to Leipzig.
1828	First composition lessons with Gottlieb Müller.
1830	Makes a piano arrangement of Beethoven's *Ninth Symphony*. Attends Thomas-Schule in Leipzig.
1831	Composition lessons with Theodor Weinlig.
1834	Finishes opera *Die Feen*.
1836	Finishes opera *Das Liebesverbot*. Marries Minna Planer.
1837	Travels to Riga and takes post as a conductor. Cosima, daughter of Franz Liszt and Countess d'Agoult born.
1839	Loses post in Riga. Flees creditors to Russia, London and Paris.
1840	Finishes *Rienzi* in Paris. Meets Liszt for the first time.
1841	Finishes *Der fliegende Holländer*.
1842	Moves to Dresden. First performance of *Rienzi* in Dresden. Begins work on *Tannhäuser*.
1843	First performance of *Der fliegende Holländer* in Dresden. Appointed Saxon Court Conductor.
1844	Weber's remains brought from London to Dresden.
1845	Finishes *Tannhäuser*. Writes prose sketch of *Die Meistersinger von Nürnberg*. Writes prose sketch for *Lohengrin*. First performance of *Tannhäuser* in Dresden.

1848 Mother dies.
Finishes *Lohengrin*.
Writes prose sketch for the future *Der Ring des Nibelungen*.
Writes poem of *Siegfrieds Tod*.

1849 Writes sketch for *Jesus von Nazareth*.
Actively involved in Dresden uprising.
Escapes a police warrant, to Liszt in Weimar, then Switzerland.

1850 First performance of *Lohengrin* in Weimar under Liszt.

1851 In Zurich, writes poem of *Der junge Siegfried*.

1852 Meets Otto and Mathilde Wesendonck for the first time.
Writes poem of *Die Walküre*.
Writes poem of *Das Rheingold*.

1853 Dedicates piano music to Mathilde Wesendonck.
Begins composition of *Das Rheingold*.
Meets Cosima Liszt in Paris for the first time.

1854 In Zurich, begins composition of *Die Walküre*.
Finishes *Das Rheingold*.
First ideas about *Tristan und Isolde*.

1855 Gives concerts in London.

1856 In Switzerland, finishes *Die Walküre*.
Writes prose sketch for *Die Sieger*.
Begins composition of *Siegfried*.

1857 First ideas about *Parsifal*.
Moves to the Asyl in the grounds of Villa Wesendonck, Zurich.
Breaks off work on *Siegfried* at the end of Act Two.
Begins work on *Tristan und Isolde* and the *Wesendonck Lieder*.
Hans von Bülow and Cosima married. Honeymoon with the Wagners.

1858 Minna intercepts letter from Wagner to Mathilde Wesendonck.
Minna leaves for a health cure.
Wagner travels to Venice.

1859 Returns to Lucerne.
Finishes *Tristan und Isolde*.
Travels to Paris. Minna joins him.

1860 Allowed to return to Germany, other than Saxony.

1861 Hostile reception to *Tannhäuser* in Paris.

1862 Travels to Biebrich in the Rhineland. Minna joins him, then leaves.
Full amnesty granted by the King of Saxony.

1863 Conducts in Vienna, Prague, St Petersburg and Moscow.
Visits the Bülows in Berlin. Relationship with Cosima grows.

1864 Serious financial problems.
Meets King Ludwig II of Bavaria who provides for his debts and makes available a house on Lake Starnberg.
Cosima visits. Bülow arrives later.
Wagner moves to Munich.

1865 Isolde, the first child of Wagner and Cosima born in Munich.
First performance of *Tristan* in Munich, conducted by Bülow.
Scandal over Wagner's private life and Ludwig's financial support.
Moves to Switzerland.

1866 Minna dies in Dresden.
Wagner moves into Haus Tribschen on Lake Lucerne at the King's expense. Cosima joins him.

1867 Eva, second child of Wagner and Cosima born at Tribschen.
Finishes *Die Meistersinger von Nürnberg*.

1868 First performance of *Meistersinger* in Munich, conducted by Bülow.
After returning briefly to Bülow, Cosima and children settle at Tribschen.

1869 Wagner takes up the composition of *Siegfried* after twelve years.
Siegfried, third child of Wagner and Cosima born at Tribschen.
First performance of *Das Rheingold* in Munich, against Wagner's wishes.
Begins composition of *Götterdämmerung*.

1870 First performance of *Die Walküre* in Munich, against Wagner's wishes.
Bülow and Cosima divorced.
Wagner and Cosima married.
First performance of the *Siegfried Idyll* at Tribschen.

1871 Finishes *Siegfried*.
In Bavaria, Bayreuth Council donates land for a theatre.

1872 Foundation stone for Bayreuth theatre laid.
Travels widely in search of potential artists for a festival.

1874 King Ludwig provides financial assistance for the theatre and the building of Haus Wahnfried.
Finishes *Götterdämmerung* and the whole *Ring* cycle.

1875 Extended concert tours in aid of funds.
Produces *Tannhäuser* and *Lohengrin* in Vienna.

1876 First performance of *Der Ring des Nibelungen*, conducted by Hans Richter, opens the Bayreuth Festspiele.

1877 Conducts concerts in London to raise funds.
Considers emigrating to America.

1882 Finishes *Parsifal* in Palermo.
First performance of *Parsifal* in Bayreuth, conducted by Hermann Levi.
Travels with family to Venice.

1883 Dies in Venice on 13 February.

Further Reading

This list identifies books that have been of particular assistance to the author. Many of these books contain detailed bibliographies from which forays may be made into the enormous resources of Wagner scholarship.

Wagner and *Parsifal*

Wagner, Richard, *My Life*, ed. M. Gregor-Dellin (Munich), trans. A. Gray, ed. M. Whittall, Cambridge, 1983.

Prose Works, trans. William Ashton Ellis (1893-98), reprinted in facsimile in 4 vols. as *Pilgrimage to Beethoven and other Essays* (1994), *Religion and Art* (1994), *Judaism in Music and other Essays* (1995) and *Opera and Drama* (1995), Bison Books, University of Nebraska Press.

Wagner, Cosima, *The Diaries 1869-1883*, 2 Vols. ed. M. Gregor-Dellin and D. Mack (Munich 1976–7); Eng. trans. G. Skelton, New York, Harcourt, Brace, Jovanovich, 1978–80.

Blunt, W. *The Dream King*, Penguin 1973.

Gilman, S.L., *Conversations with Nietzsche*, trans. D.J. Parent, Oxford University Press, 1987.

Gutman, R., *Richard Wagner, The Man, His Mind and His Music*, Secker and Warburg, 1968.

Millington, Barry, ed., *The Wagner Compendium*, Thames and Hudson, 1992.

Newman, Ernest, *Wagner Nights*, Putnam, 1949, Pan Books, 1977.

The Life of Richard Wagner, 4 vols. London, New York, Alfred A. Knopf, 1933–47.

Nietzsche, Friedrich, *The Birth of Tragedy* (1872), trans. Walter Kaufmann, New York, Vintage, 1967.

Human, All Too Human (1878), trans. R.J. Hollingdale, Cambridge University Press, 1986.

The Case of Wagner (1888), trans. Walter Kaufmann, New York, Vintage, 1967.

Nietzsche contra Wagner, in *The Portable Nietzsche* (1888), trans. Walter Kaufmann, New York, Viking, 1968.

Spotts, F., *Bayreuth, A History of the Wagner Festival*, Yale University Press, 1994.

Tanner, Michael, *Nietzsche*, Oxford University Press, 1994.

Taylor, R., *Richard Wagner, His Life, Art and Thought*, Paul Elek, London, 1979.

The Grail, Medieval Romances and Medieval History

Chrétien de Troyes, *Perceval, or, The story of the Grail*; trans. Ruth Harwood Cline, Pergamon Press, 1983.

Wolfram von Eschenbach, *Parzival*; trans. A.T. Hatto, Penguin, 1980.

Sir Thomas Malory, *Le Morte D'Arthur* (2 vols.); ed. Janet Cowan; intro. John Lawlor, Penguin Classics, 1969.

Campbell, Joseph, *The Masks of God: Creative Mythology*, London, Secker and Warburg, 1968.

Jung, Emma and Marie-Louise von Franz, *The Grail Legend*, trans. Andrea Dykes, 2nd edn., Princeton University Press, 1998.

Woodhouse, F.C., *The Military Religious Orders of the Middle Ages*, London, Society for Promoting Christian Knowledge, 1879.

Schopenhauer, Buddhism and Brahmanism

Gardiner, Patrick, *Schopenhauer*, Pelican, 1967.

Magee, Bryan, *The Philosophy of Schopenhauer*, Oxford University Press, 1983, revised 1997.

The Teachings of Buddha, compiled by Paul Carus, Rider, 1998.

Buddhist Scriptures, selected and trans. Edward Conze, Penguin, 1959.

Gethin, Rupert, *The Foundations of Buddhism*, Oxford University Press, 1998.

Thich Nhat Hanh, *Old Path White Clouds*, trans. Mobi Ho, Berkeley, California, Parallax Press, 1991.

Index

Wakefield Press has been publishing good Australian books
for over fifty years. For a catalogue of current and
forthcoming titles, or to add your name to our mailing list,
send your name and address to

Wakefield Press, Box 2266, Kent Town, South Australia 5071.
Telephone: (08) 8362 8800 Fax: (08) 8362 7592
Web: www.wakefieldpress.com.au

WIRRA WIRRA VINEYARDS

ARTSA

Wakefield Press thanks Wirra Wirra Vineyards and
Arts South Australia for their continued support.